OFFICE AUTOMATION

OFFICE

AUTOMATION

George R. Terry, Ph.D.

Consultant in Management
Chicago, Illinois

1966

Dow Jones-Irwin, Inc.

Homewood, Illinois

First printing, July, 1966
Second printing, March, 1969

LIBRARY OF CONGRESS CATALOG CARD NO. 66–24596
PRINTED IN THE UNITED STATES OF AMERICA

INTRODUCTION

AUTOMATION in the office is becoming commonplace and is steadily and surely advancing into a dominant position in performing office work. The evolution taking place in the office is at times almost unbelievable. The processing of paperwork today presents an entirely different picture from that of just a decade ago. And promises of things to come in this area stagger the imagination.

The purpose of *Office Automation* is to present the essential background and the current practices of automation in the office so that necessary paperwork is accomplished effectively. New practices proving superior are gaining rapid favor; the meaning of what is necessary paperwork is being greatly modified; and getting the work accomplished with the least time, effort, and cost remains the chief stabilizer of the total effort.

The writing is from the informative viewpoint; both managers and nonmanagers can profit from the basic material presented. The latest developments are described and the significance of these developments is pointed out. The goal has been a concise, practical presentation that is nontechnical, yet complete. Illustrations and charts are numerous to expedite understanding of the material.

The book is intended for every member of management—at the top, middle, or bottom level; for line or staff member, systems analyst, procedures designer, data collector or processor, clerical employee, teacher, practitioner, or student; for everyone interested in knowing more about the fascinating and all encompassing area of office automation.

This interesting, fast-moving, challenging, and somewhat disturbing subject area has sharpened the focus upon data and their processing. Having adequate facts and figures is being emphasized now more than ever before. The trend is toward more immediate, more accurate data. Greater mechanization, new improvements of computers, better means and more widespread usage of processed data, are the order of the day. The changes are directly or indirectly affecting everyone. Indeed, it is difficult to overstress the importance of office automation.

Developments of the computer are thoughts that quickly come to mind when the subject, automation in the office, is mentioned. Visions of a completely automated office, an automated factory, automated warehouse, automated train—even an automated world—stir our mental impulses.

What does the latest computer do? How does one communicate with it? How can it help me? These are typical questions. Understanding of the computer is sought and it is essential.

But the movement toward automation in the office has given rise not only to the importance of the computer, but also to an entirely new office technology. This movement, spearheaded by the advent of the computer, has altered the entire concept of office work and how it is processed. The movement has changed our concepts and tools for structuring the work, has provided much greater recognition to the interrelatedness of all records and reports, and has emphasized information essentiality and its place in modern enterprises. In addition, the dynamics has greatly influenced the design and use of so-called ordinary office equipment and machines as well as the managerial approaches in handling office work. In other words, while the coming "push-button" age is being accelerated by the computer, its contributions are not confined only to its technical and direct role.

A total of nine chapters make up this book. The material is organized to expedite understanding; a logical and inclusive pattern is followed. The beginning chapter deals with the new office technology movement and is an introduction to important automated ways for accomplishing office work. Following this, the systems and procedures approach to office automation is discussed. The need for structuring the concept of the data to be automated, the importance of systems and procedures in automation, and the possible future contribution of this approach are discussed in some detail. Next, the fundamentals of processing office work are presented, followed by a discussion of the common office equipment and machines that are available. Following this, in Chapter 6, source data automation is discussed. This is automation accomplished by joining common office machines together so that they operate as an integrated mass. We can also process the office work by means of the computer. In this respect, technical considerations are presented in Chapter 7, and managerial considerations in Chapter 8. The last chapter, Chapter 9, deals with selected and informative applications of computers.

I am indebted to many for help in preparing this book. The exchange of ideas, the sharing of information, and the encouragement received from others have contributed immensely. Appreciation is extended to associates, clients, manufacturers of office equipment and machines, and friends for their help, interest, and cooperation.

Chicago
June, 1966   GEORGE R. TERRY

TABLE OF CONTENTS

CHAPTER ONE

THE NEW OFFICE

TECHNOLOGY

The wise man does at once what the fool does finally.
—Gracian

WE ARE moving into a new world much faster than most of us realize. Spaceships zoom in the vastness of the universe. Supersonic airliners will soon fly men at speeds of 2,000 miles an hour. Trains are being designed to go at speeds of 200 miles an hour. And at this moment, scientists are probing under the ocean nearly ten miles deep for minerals and the unknown. These developments are all a part of the greatest research program in the history of mankind.

This pace of progress has stimulated efforts to develop machines and hasten their application to office work because information is so essential to all activities and especially to research and development. Significant office technological advances have been won, yet even greater things to come are predicted. Routine office jobs are being eliminated, office work is being accomplished at fantastic speeds, and the makeup of office work is undergoing significant changes.

DEFINITION OF OFFICE AUTOMATION

To most of us, the term "office technology" brings to mind office automation. The word "automation" first appeared in print about 1948. Since that time, this word has stimulated much discussion and controversy; it has been accorded many different meanings. Some consider automation as a synonym for technological change, while others believe it denotes mechanization. Commonly, the word is used solely in connection with the processing of products in a factory; but, while popular, this concept

1

is obviously incomplete, since data processing and the compilation of information have been subjected to technological improvements.

In performing work of any kind, automation normally means the arrangement whereby one or more machines are operated without human participation except to press the starter button. It is the regulation of processing by which high-speed, self-correcting instruments or machines control the operations of other machines. In a very real sense, automation is the extension of mechanization. If an office machine can be operated and controlled by other machines or devices, office automation can be said to exist. The situation, however, is primarily one of degree and terminology.

To comprehend fully office automation as it currently exists, it is helpful to understand its various components. As will be pointed out in subsequent chapters in some detail, the format of the work to be done is conceived via the media of systems and procedures. This sets the stage and defines the objectives as well as the constraints. Also to a significant degree, the use of some present-day office machines, other than computers, is commonly referred to as office automation. Hence, it is necessary to include office machines other than computers in a discussion of office automation. In fact, these noncomputer machines can be integrated or joined to form a data processing unit—one which provides for all intents and purposes an automated arrangement. The use of computers, of course, is synonymous with the meaning of office automation and is fully discussed in the latter part of this book.

Office automation relieves mankind of menial work. Most office work requires some human cerebration; but when the work is repetitive in nature or subject to exact formulation, it can be effectively handled by machine. By such means, man is free to employ his mind for work which the human brain *alone* can encompass.

ILLUSTRATIONS OF THE NEW OFFICE TECHNOLOGY

It is no exaggeration to state that nearly every office task can be automated by the application of electronics, electrostatics, magnetics, or pneumatics. Scientific breakthroughs are speeding the accomplishments of the new office technology. For example, now available are electrostatic printing units capable of printing 72 million characters an hour—or of printing this entire book in less than two minutes. It is now possible in digital form to record magnetically on a square inch of tape the words contained on four pages of this book and, further, to process this amount of information at a rate of 40 pages per second. Machines can multiply two 13-digit figures in 31 millionths of a second, that is, at the rate of

32,000 such multiplications in one second. Work is now being perfected to achieve the amazing reduction of 160,000 to 1 for filming information. This means that the entire contents of three books like the one you are now reading could be recorded on a single film smaller than the size of an ordinary post card. The contents of an entire library could be kept in an ordinary card file.

As indicated above, the new office technology is actually a part of the great technological advances being applied to every branch of industry, and the trend is toward new and better machines. Applications in the factory, in sales, in research, in medicine, in the military, and in transportation are giving greater impetus to the growth in importance of paper work and to its processing in keeping with developments in these other areas. For example, an oil refinery, completely automated, requires only three men to operate the control buttons. And a steel-pipe plant employing automatic machines produces four times as much pipe with one-third the number of employees formerly used. Airplanes are guided in "blind" takeoffs and landings, movements of trains can be controlled, and the course of storms can be charted and weather maps quickly sent to stations across the nation. Managers of retail stores can find which items are selling satisfactorily, which poorly, which items to discontinue, which to promote, which to purchase, and where to display (shelf and location in store), all by means of a point-of-purchase analysis rapidly calculated by an electronic office machine. In another application, voluminous data on the buying habits of soft drink purchasers in a given sales territory are fed into a computer, in addition to data on the composition of newspaper and television audiences in this same territory. Within minutes the most efficient combination of media for a given advertising budget is calculated by the computer.

SCOPE OF THE NEW OFFICE TECHNOLOGY

The boundaries of the new office technology appear limitless. The advances are neither confined to any one subject area nor to any one type of enterprise. In fact, they defy any arbitrary lines of demarcation. Equipment exists and is operable to take advantage of the new technology. What holds us back or restrains our adoption of the new technology is our limited vision, imagination, and decisiveness. The major issue is basic, not to the type of equipment, but to the managers.

Knowing the kinds of information needed to manage and operate a given enterprise is fundamental. For example, answers to these questions are necessary: What information do you need to know? In what format should it be? How accurate? How frequent? Who should be given all or a part of this information? What do we need to know to plan effectively? How much controlling is needed? Should we emphasize centralization or decentralization in our organizing efforts? To answer these questions requires the ability to determine what information is important, and, once obtaining it, how it will be used. In this connection an understanding of both the nature of the enterprise and its activities is valuable.

To take full advantage of the office technology's offerings, we should also know what specific activities give rise to the information needed to manage the enterprise. Not all activities generate information of equal value. Concentrating our efforts on the really important ones, we can then

Purpose of Information	*Common Media*	*For Managerial Activity*
To forecast business conditions	Plans	Planning
To allocate resources	Programs	Planning
To schedule time use	Reports	Controlling
To determine quantity	Reports	Controlling
To determine quality	Reports	Controlling
To establish standards	Reports and Manuals	Controlling
To evaluate performance against standards	Records and Reports	Controlling
To inform employees, customers, and stockholders	Letters and Bulletins	Actuating
To fulfill commitments to customers and suppliers	Records and Letters	Actuating
To meet governmental requirements	Reports	Controlling

FIG 1. The purpose, media, and for what fundamental managerial activity information is utilized.

find out pertinent facts about these key activities, facts such as the channels through which this key information flows, what departments receive it, and what departments use it.

Knowing for a given enterprise the information essential for its management and where this information is generated, it is then possible to localize problem areas where there is need for help, and the manner of performing the work in this area can be improved by utilizing more efficient data processing. In other words, an effort is made to match the places where there is a real need for improvement with the places where it is believed help can be supplied.

Figure 1 gives a brief summary of selected important information for management purposes. The list is suggestive only. Data for planning purposes are sought and emphasized to achieve better decision making. The possibility of supplying an inclusive background and of analyzing a wide range of alternatives makes planning information valuable. Likewise, control types of information supply a manager with important data, particularly when the information is almost instantaneous with the occurrence of the activity. Production, inventory, and sales are major areas where current control information is essential.

WHY AUTOMATE?

Managers of present-day enterprises need considerable data to help them make effective decisions. As the managerial need for information becomes more and more pressing, the means for supplying this information quickly and completely have been stimulated. This is reason No. 1 why companies automate their data-processing work. In the quick tempo of today, events affecting enterprises seem to occur with increasing rapidity, and many decisions must take into account at least part of these events. Under such conditions, the gathering, processing, and distributing of data must be done as quickly as possible. In certain areas, the tremendous amounts of paper work required can be handled within a reasonable period only by machine. In the case of supplying scientific and research data calculated from mathematical formulas, a machine accomplishes in several hours what would require years of manual calculation.

A second major reason for office automation is to reduce office costs. In some instances, this goal is achieved; but in others, cost reduction is more fancy than fact. One is inclined to believe that in any installation, because of the speed and versatility of office machines used in automation, paperwork costs are reduced. Unfortunately, it is difficult to make accurate comparisons of a "before and after" office automation. Usually, many innovations are effected by automation. The report requirements may change, due mainly to these innovations; and the volume of work may increase, since the processing time is stepped up and "we have the necessary machines." Also, some of the departmental operations may undergo transitions of one type or another. If all factors remained on a status quo basis before and after automation, and there is an adequate volume of work, the costs under automation will be reduced. But a condition that very likely develops is more data processing with approximately the same dollar expenditure.

This does not mean that office automation is not an attractive investment. Quite the contrary, it usually is a good investment; otherwise, managers would not utilize it. A well-planned, -installed, and -managed installation will return a saving of approximately 30–40 percent on the total investment each year. To achieve this return, it is necessary in many cases to operate the equipment five days a week, sixteen hours a day. In each case, individual circumstances govern and must be taken into account for the particular conditions present.

An important reason for office automation frequently overlooked is reduction of errors. Machines seldom commit mistakes; and when they do, it usually is the fault of the person operating them. Office automation tends to integrate data processing and thus minimizes the number of times the data are handled; hence, it reduces the possibilities of committing errors. Higher-quality office work can be viewed as a by-product, even though it is an important contribution of office automation.

In addition, the office work force represents one of the fastest growing groups in our economy. The search for competent office help is continuous. Ways of getting out the necessary work with a limited number of people have been eagerly sought, or an arrangement requiring employment of only the more competent office employees has won favor. Both these conditions are met by automating office work. In many cases, the capacity of the automated system is greater than current needs; and as the clerical work load increases, it will not be necessary to add people, but rather the system can be depended upon to take on most of the additional load. This assures adequate clerical help for perhaps the next decade.

The last reason to be discussed is the desire to have an internal status symbol. Automating office work signifies progress; and in some instances, it appears that equipment was ordered and installed simply because certain executives insisted upon having it. Whether the type and amount of equipment were adequate and proper for their needs was hastily reviewed, and full utilization of the equipment has never been made. Instances of this nature are relatively minor, yet they demonstrate that the basis of some automation is impulsive and personal, not rational and logical.

THE FEASIBILITY OF AUTOMATION

Automating the paper work of an enterprise can be a detailed and complicated task. For best results, it is imperative that the entire cycle of the work to be automated be taken into account, that the real objectives be carefully defined and used as guides in designing the manner of work performance, and that the proper equipment be selected and employed for the intended use. Actually, two aspects of data processing are involved: (1) the makeup of the paper work itself and (2) the processing of the data as such. Under the former are included the design of the entire cycle, what data are included, in what form, to what form, and how utilized. Under the second point are the actual uses of the equipment typically operating on a continuing basis. These two aspects of data processing are interrelated, and the experts in each area should work together as a team, with each aware of the other's problems.

In some "feasibility" studies, the erroneous assumption is made that office automation is desirable regardless of the current work performance mode. The result is that inefficiencies in paper work are automated or some data are permitted to remain in a form which is incompatible with best automation practices. As a result, both the good and the bad features of the present manner of doing the work are preserved. Experience clearly demonstrates that it is extremely difficult to remove unnecessary data or to change basic procedures once they are incorporated in the office automation arrangement. In fact, a computer when misused is probably the finest device in the world for sealing in existing deficiencies. The proper approach is to conduct a thorough and sound study prior to the decision to use any form of automation. Only in this way is a solid and reliable foundation established for all the subsequent phases of improvement, simplification, and mechanization.

What is included in a thorough and sound study? A number of considerations, including the objectives of the enterprise and the contributions expected of each functional area or organizational unit to the achievement of these objectives. The decision-making activity vested in each management member should be clearly identified so that the information needs of each member can be determined. Familiarity with the organization structure assists in answering who decides what, who is expected to inform whom, and what information is needed. Generally, it is also helpful to know the relative importance of the various basic functions of the enterprise—manufacturing, marketing, financing, engineering, and personnel—in order to obtain some impression of the probable characteristics of the data to be handled. Also, any future increased work loads and contemplated changes should be taken into account, as well as the existing means of performing the work, no matter how primitive, because such facts can have an important bearing upon the recommendations.

Sometimes the term "feasibility of automation" is erroneously interpreted to mean the possible or probable adoption or success of an enterprise in utilizing data-processing equipment. Office automation is a reality. The question to be answered is not the degree of success predicted for certain equipment, but an evaluation of equipment alternatives based on resultant costs, time in process, flexibility of usage, and ability to meet future requirements. A number of different types of office machines can perform the work. For any individual user the question is: Which one will do my paper work best in keeping with my personal needs?

To be sure, equipment manufacturers have developed standardized, practical, and economical ways of processing certain data. We might refer to them as "standardized paper work programs." The processing of payrolls, accounts payable, and purchasing are examples. These can be handled fairly uniformly in company after company, but in many cases they are not, and for any number of reasons. On the other hand, paper work dealing with budgeting, material control, and sales control varies considerably from enterprise to enterprise, presumably because of company size, practices of the business, characteristics of the enterprise, the overall objectives, the product, the service, and personal preference. Consequently they are evaluated individually in many feasibility studies.

Also, too much emphasis may be placed on the practicality or desirability of utilizing particular types of machines and equipment. Attention is focused on speeds, peak loads, scheduling, and other technical considerations. While these are important, it must also be remembered that the data are being processed for utilization, to help somebody do his job better because of the processed data provided to him. Furthermore, concentrating on the processing of the data per se may result in inadequate consideration for such things as acquiring the source data, converting the data into suitable form for machine processing, supplying the processed information in the best format, and getting it to the right personnel at the right time.

CHANGES IN MANAGEMENT STRUCTURE

One of the most important effects of the new office technology upon the management structure is the increased emphasis given to taking a broader viewpoint or perspective of the entirety, rather than of one single component. The trend of developments appears to be toward the swiftest possible reaction by an *entire* enterprise to any given stimulus. The enterprise is being viewed more and more as a responsive body instead of a cluster of individual and, to some extent, isolated departments. In the future, the work of the office manager will be carried out in more sweeping yet integrated lines. The management of information should be viewed as an activity affecting all parts of an enterprise, and areas outside the enterprise as well. The trend of managerial thinking is definitely toward this broader concept. For example, we are now considering paper work efforts not just within a definite small work center, or within a department, but within several departments or the entire enterprise. To illustrate, Figure 2 has been included. Here, for the study of informational requirements, the entire enterprise is considered a unit. Certain data, termed *input,* are fed into the unit. They include such data as customers' orders, price information from vendors, and information on special technical processes. Within the unit, or the enterprise, the input data are processed, some are retained and some are issued or fed out as *output* data. Price quotations to customers, sales, shipments, and bank checks for payables are illustrative of output data. In addition, the figure includes the concept called *feedback*. This is a selected portion of the *output* used to control for either self-supervision or modification of further processing.[1]

Another effect of the new technology upon the management structure is the emergence of a management information group or department. Such a group will probably become more and more common and will occupy a relatively high organizational level. As office automation increases and experience in obtaining full utilization of office technology is acquired,

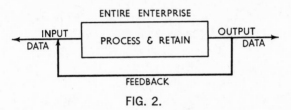

FIG. 2.

fuller integration of information will be accomplished. This, in turn, will mean less paper work and reports by personnel of the operating departments. Supervisors, for example, will not be required to spend two to three hours daily on paper work. This shift will enable employees to devote more of their time to their primary function. Also, it is quite likely that a reduction in the size of the clerical staff groups of the operating departments could result. To illustrate, sales analysis of sales and labor costs of production might well be transferred to the information center.

For a given office, automation usually increases relatively the machine cost and decreases the labor cost. In turn, the greater machine expenditure spotlights attention upon questions of depreciation; scheduling and maintaining even work flows, and keeping the mechanized units in top working condition; utilization of records; and format of reports. Automation in the office stresses managerial problems; in the factory, the problems are primarily technical.

Office technology influences the management structure, not only of the large company, but also of the small one. The present and relatively limited routine processing performed by a service bureau for small companies will probably expand to cover more encompassing areas.[2]

---

[1] There will be much more discussion about the breadth and approach to office work in the next two chapters.

[2] A service bureau performs office work for a client at a fee. The service is usually excellent. Typically, service bureaus are located in major cities, specialize in given work areas, and offer wide experience and "know-how" in their selective fields of operation.

Equipment considerations alone will not bring this about, but the scarcity of competent and experienced analytical talent will make the service bureau arrangement the logical choice of the small enterprise.

CONFUSION ABOUT OFFICE TECHNOLOGY

Several factors constitute major obstacles to the complete understanding and utilization of contributions available from office technology developments. These factors include (1) the overemphasis upon technical details, (2) the lack of adequately trained personnel, (3) the adoption of special jargon, and (4) the basically divergent viewpoints or philosophies taken toward computers. Let us examine each of these in some detail.

A tendency to overemphasize technical details is the source of much chaos. To the average layman the need is for what the equipment will do for him rather than how it does it. For some, the "how" is intriguing, but appreciation and use of an automobile, for example, does not necessitate knowing precisely how the thousand separate parts operate. Some people must know all the details, but most people who are involved in the "computer age" are neither technicians nor do they want to be. However, some technical data are essential and should be provided. But too much regard for how the data are processed can result in too little regard for what kinds of data are being provided. The data processing becomes an end in itself rather than a means to an end.

Every emerging new field of endeavor suffers from the lack of trained personnel. The office technology is no exception. We have a tendency to minimize the importance of people in office automation. The equipment is in the spotlight, it receives the publicity and glamour. But trained people are needed to design the process and to operate the machines. In certain companies the overflow from other departments has formed the basis for personnel used in the office automation unit, that is, the unit consists chiefly of discarded or reassigned employees. Apparently not much effort has been made to recruit and train new, young, highly intelligent, and proficient people for these vital office jobs. Competent managerial skill is also in short supply. Fantastic office machines are in operation, but in a number of cases management of them leaves much to be desired. All the office equipment in the world falls short of its potential unless we have the manpower to manage it effectively.

Office technology has developed its own jargon. To the newcomer it is comprised of strange terminology unlike anything previously encountered. Words like bit, binary number, access time, real-time, buffer, program, and storage take on special meanings quite different from those previously associated with them. Furthermore, there is confusion about the meaning of certain basic words. Hence, the same word doesn't always have the same meaning. Obviously, this state of affairs makes for difficulties in communication. A sales manager may attempt to learn the intricacies of electronic data processing but become discouraged by the specialized and somewhat stilted language of the technical books recommended to him. Or he may find it a real chore to communicate with the executive in charge of computer activities. In contrast, data-processing personnel encounter difficulty in presenting ideas to sales management personnel. A common complaint of the processor is that he "just can't get through to top and middle managers."

Lastly, confusion about office technology results from widely divergent viewpoints about its identity and contribution. At one extreme is the belief that electronic data processing applies primarily to clerical types of applications, and that this work should be neatly tucked within a well-known major organizational unit such as finance or production where it can be given the proper orientation. In contrast, others contend that electronic data processing includes all types of operations—clerical, production process controls, and engineering problem solving. They look upon computers as highly sophisticated processors of data limited only by man's ingenuity and imagination. Further, they believe that because of its tremendous capacities and possibilities, with information lines cutting across traditional organization lines, the computer should be located in an information center or department reporting to the top executive. These two viewpoints are the extremes of a spectrum which includes many variations between the two limits. Companies have enjoyed benefits by following either of these viewpoints; the approach is not a measure of success. The point here is that divergent viewpoints are present and they condition the use and status of electronic data processing.

CHALLENGES OF NEW OFFICE TECHNOLOGY

The uses of new techniques and machines to supply needed information multiply daily, and so do the users. The trend is unquestionably upward, whether measured by casual observation, surveys, statements of managers, or the number of office machines in use. Computer manufacturers, for example, now do an annual business of nearly $1½ billion. With this growth, management members are making bigger demands on the office because of the needs for specific information. The effect is to give the manager in charge of information a much larger scope of operations, much more opportunity, and much greater responsibility.

For the most part, basic issues pertaining to data processing are the reflection of basic issues of management. The computer, for example, cannot be viewed as an autonomous "black box" that will solve in some ingenious manner the headaches of managers. The computer is an adjunct to management; its role is to supply information to managers so that they can do their jobs better. But managers have to know their requirements, achieve a clarity of thought, and develop precise plans in order to obtain satisfactory results from a computer. Modern electronic data processing emphasizes the importance of management. Success with automated information efforts depends mainly upon the understanding which managers can and do bring in communicating with processors. Managers must be able to identify corporate objectives and advise of changes when these objectives shift.

One of the outstanding challenges of the new office technology is to improve existent information by streamlining old means of processing essential information into a format that stimulates effective usage of the information. To this end, the office manager should capture the initiative and suggest what types and arrangements of information might be of greatest assistance to the recipient. Too frequently, it is assumed that identical information and reports should continue after automation as existed before automation. The common practice of asking the recipient what information he wants usually results in a continuation of the existent information because the recipient does not know what other types he might have or how what he is receiving might be bettered. In short, he is not an expert in designing the information needs and report structure of his company. Perhaps no one man is—or for that matter, no one group; but certainly, efforts of reasonably skilled people in this area will assist in achieving better information.

An illustration will demonstrate the challenge of information improvement in the typical enterprise, which improvement can usually be won during the time of office automation installation. In a well-known company headquartered in Boston, the vice-president of finance is provided on a monthly basis with information on (1) items having a nonrecurring profit impact, (2) items having a continuing profit impact, and (3) financial managerial subjects requiring policy determination or modification. Such information differs from the rigid and common standardized financial data, yet it provides valuable assistance in vital decision making concerning financial matters.

Various studies among companies regarding their computer installations reveal specific areas for improvement. A rather common occurrence is a lack of determining corporate requirements. Emphasis is placed on data of a certain department rather than on interdepartmental or total operational information. Also, improper or inadequate planning is done resulting in ill-timed crash programs and scheduling difficulties. A complaint of many companies is that the conversion to the computer takes too long. Operations are unduly disrupted, jams occur in the work flow, and the entire mode of work accomplishment is upset.

OFFICE AUTOMATION AND MANAGERIAL DECISION MAKING

Among the greatest influences of the new office technology is its effect upon managerial decision making. There are three major effects to consider:

1. *It aids in establishing a more sound basis for managerial decision making.* Modern office technology makes it economically feasible to compile data on a current basis. A manager can now know where he is rather than where he has been. To make decisions, reliance need not be placed on facts conditioned by the old traditional lags in information. Furthermore, it is possible to relate different units of measurement regarding company activities. No longer need production reports be expressed as units stamped per day, or shift, and inventory in some other measurement unit. The entire fund of information can be in a measuring unit common and meaningful to all concerned departments. Also, all the interrelated data can be of a comparable time period. For example, the period and frequencies for production reports can be precisely identical to those of inventory, or of sales reports. Thus, valid correlation of the information can be calculated.

2. *It makes feasible the use of new analytical techniques in managerial decision making.* Mathematics has long been applied to engineering and production problems, but it is now being utilized in management decision-making problems. The significant relationships of the important factors are determined and related mathematically. Then, different values for the variable factors are substituted in the equation and tentative answers calculated. In this way, the best combination of factors for the most desirable answer is determined. In the past, the physical inability of clerical staffs to process all relevant information according to the limits prescribed by the mathematical equation made it impractical to determine many alternative decisions under different sets or conditions or factors. The techniques employed depend upon the problem and conditions under which the factors must operate. Among the more common techniques are linear programming, queuing theory, games theory, and optimization formulas.

3. *It makes possible the pretesting of decisions by means of simulation.* Office automation makes it physically possible to solve tomorrow's problem today, before a real crisis develops. Simulation includes the building of a model of a company that behaves exactly like the real thing;

in other words, this model reflects actual operating conditions. Different tentative decisions are followed through to their respective different answers—what would happen as a result of each solution. The best answer can then be selected from various alternatives, and the decision to make for this desired answer is identified.

Simulation provides the answers to "what if" questions. It is made practical through office automation, which can solve problems that are too complex and have too many variables to solve through human effort alone. However, the use of a model to acquire knowledge is nothing new. Engineers have used this technique for years. Models of new designs are constructed and subsequently subjected to varying conditions of operation in order to determine the design providing optimum favorable results. In like manner, the manager using simulation does the same thing.

HOW MUCH OFFICE AUTOMATION?

Decisions involving office automation are matters of importance to every enterprise. The proper amount or degree of office automation varies somewhat with the circumstance primarily because the meaning of automation is not constant. Automation is not a single entity. It might be the application of a computer to production control or a punched card adopted for handling orders between a factory and several warehouses. It is never accomplished in the sense that further progress in data processing is not possible.

No office is completely automated. Even though technologically possible, at least in the conceptual stage, the fully automated office is not *economically* feasible. And it is the economics of each situation that is a strong determinant of the degree to which automation proceeds. The best current estimates are that some 35–40 percent of the total office work is performed by electronic means in the typical present-day automated office, but it might well be higher. Certainly office automation as we recognize it today is not an office made up of 100 percent robots.

Of particular importance is the achieving of the best correlation between the demands made on the information system and the physical equipment itself. This involves the danger of overmechanization or of undermechanization in the office. From this problem of optimum fit stem many automation difficulties. For example, the equipment may turn out to be too elaborate for the specific company's needs, thus making the equipment investment excessive. Or frequent and expensive breakdowns may occur primarily because too much work or too many different types of work are being attempted with the particular machines. In other cases, the installation cost may greatly exceed estimates—a condition commonly arising from inadequate analysis of necessary informational demands.

Another problem is to determine specifically what work is and what work is not to be done by the machines. Some work is best done by a willing hand and a pencil, especially when the cost of operating the machine is taken into account. Likewise, a policy of charging each department for the machine time of a centralized unit can have the effect of loading too much work on the machine. This comes about quite innocently, in that a department head charged with a machine cost customarily sees to it that he gets something in return. Net result: Some work which should not be handled by the center is sent there for processing. The remedy lies in educating every management member to the economic considerations and limitations of each piece of office equipment and to the idea of total information integration.

In contrast, some offices are not mechanized enough, a state of affairs which commonly arises from indifference, fear, ignorance, or lack of direction or capital. The attitude of "Let us alone; we've been doing it this way since 1930" is one of the chief contributors to this condition. Seldom do office employees demand mechanization or hover around the machine, praising it, after installation. Their normal reaction is not to make any changes. Also, ignorance and the lack of well-defined directions by top managers can lead to undermechanization. Failure to perceive the broad implications of office automation and personal preference for other areas may be cited as the major reasons for this lack of needed direction. In addition, lack of capital may be responsible, but this is a somewhat dubious reason because most installations pay for themselves quickly and easy financing terms are readily available from the equipment seller.

SOCIAL ASPECTS OF OFFICE AUTOMATION

Social change stimulated by office automation emphasizes employment modifications, which can be viewed as offering either (1) greater opportunities or (2) fewer opportunities, even to the point of mass unemployment. The former is indicative of the attitude under which office automation will come to maturity. It stresses: "What will automation help us do better, or assist us to achieve that has never been achieved?" There is a problem, however, in adapting to this greater opportunity. In this connection, much human effort will shift from manual to mental work and from menial to more challenging tasks. Automation puts at our disposal the means to a materially more abundant life. In the second viewpoint, the dominant force is fear. Employees are quite naturally concerned whether the higher rates of office work performance will result in unemployment or in raising living standards. Past experience seems to indicate that technological advancements have increased the overall level of employment. New demands have developed, the machines themselves creating a large labor force required for their construction and maintenance. However, many people are *displaced,* not *replaced* to other areas of duty. For example, a large installation of electronic office machines in a Chicago office required the shifting of several hundred employees to other jobs. Not a one lost his job; each was trained and placed in new work. This called for real management ability and, of course, necessitated an adjustment on the part of each employee.

To the opponents of office automation the blunt question may be directed: What is the alternative to office automation? The answer appears to be to maintain the status quo and to refrain from utilizing technological progress and faster and better ways of performing office work. Such action would downgrade our offices, our economy, and our society in general. This would be regression on a tragic scale. We would be saying to hundreds of thousands of scientists and engineers striving to advance our office technology that we don't want and will not use this additional knowledge. We must ever be mindful that progress means change and places before us broad challenges and threats which we must meet and conquer; otherwise we shall stagnate.

Many times in the office, the normal rate of attrition will bring about the smaller work force required. But older employees with seniority and relatively little flexibility pose difficulties. In a large insurance company, the personnel whose jobs were eliminated in the advance to more office automation were divided into three classes:

> The largest class includes relatively unskilled junior personnel in clerical jobs of a repetitive nature—filing, sorting, recording, and performing other tasks where only a bare minimum of insurance knowledge is required. The second class consisted of personnel with more experience, and many years of seniority, who are in relatively routine jobs which require slightly more knowledge of insurance. Jobs of this class do not require original thinking, nor judgment beyond that necessary to identify an exception to usual routine which must be passed along to higher authority for action. The third class is composed of more highly skilled people engaged in supervisory and senior staff work. Their duties are primarily in the judgment area, and they require a more advanced knowledge of insurance.[3]

The writer of this quotation goes on to say that relocation of the unskilled junior personnel and of the skilled senior people create relatively few problems. It is the experienced employee performing routine jobs not in the judgment area who presents troublesome personnel dislocation difficulties because there are few job openings for a person with these qualifications and usually such an employee is relatively inflexible.

---

[3] E. W. Martin, Jr., "Practical Problems of Introducing a Computer," *Business Horizons,* Fall, 1960, p. 8 (published by the Indiana University School of Business, Bloomington, Indiana).

Many are of the opinion that skill requirements will increase for most office jobs as a result of automation. From the overall viewpoint, this might be, but it is well to observe that many jobs of relatively low skill will remain. Certainly training and the need for proficiency in specific skills are emphasized by automation. The person with no skill is hard put to find work.

Undoubtedly, the number of irksome, monotonous tasks is reduced by automation. Much laborious and time-consuming office work is done by the machine. This is desirable from the social point of view and is a benefit to mankind. Many feel that we are at the beginning of what might be described as a second Industrial Revolution, which will substitute machines for human beings in performing mental drudgery, just as the first Industrial Revolution substituted machines for carrying out most backbreaking physical drudgery.

THINGS TO COME

It is a natural human instinct to anticipate what future progress can be expected in office management and what events of the future might change the office as we know it today. Experience of the present, although limited, suggests possible changes to be expected due to office technology. It appears fairly certain that many of the present ways of performing office work will fall by the wayside. Much of the required writing and calculating will be done automatically by machines which will operate from sound. Communicative devices will probably revolutionize the distribution of information, and it could be that most conferences will be handled on closed TV circuits or some adaptation thereof. Future reproducing processes are almost certain to establish an entirely new concept of filing and storing records. Papers common to our present office will be replaced by some medium such as electronic impulses stored in a computer. Many of these changes may not come about until many years ahead, while others may take place within the present decade.

It is reasonable to predict that decision making will be improved. The qualification of data, made possible by office improvements, will not only improve the amount and the quality of facts but will reveal pertinent relationships among them. The availability of a wider range of alternatives evaluated factually could reduce decision making based either on intuition or on historical data projection. Also, decision making will be carried out on a broader base. Company goals, not departmental goals, will be stressed; and the interaction of decisions pertaining to departments will be emphasized.

The handling of information will be carefully planned and engineered. The haphazard, "just let it grow as needs develop" attitude will decline to a minor position. Office work will become more closely related to managerial planning and controlling, and will be used to the full. The products of the office will increase in value and importance.

With all these changes, it is logical to state that an office manager's work will take on greater importance. With larger amounts of accurate and timely factual information available, the operational consequences of a decision will be measured more precisely, but the decision cannot be an automatic response to the impact of information. Judgment, consideration for nonmeasurable but influential factors, and responsibility for consequences are not transferred to the office automation equipment. They remain, at least in the foreseeable future, with the manager.

WHERE ARE WE NOW?

With all these changes, constraints, forces, and innovations in the performance of office work, the total picture presented may be a bit confusing. To summarize, we might ask, "What are the most significant

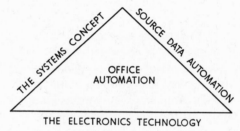

FIG. 3.   The triangle of office automation.

developments of the office technology up to the present time?" It would be easy to list some eight or ten really important changes. However, for purposes of this book, we will compress our list and select only those that are indeed extremely significant. When we do this we have three headings: (1) the systems concept, (2) source data automation (SDA), and (3) the electronics technology.

These constitute the main structural members of office automation as we know it today. They can be illustrated in the form of a triangle as shown in Figure 3. These three structural members comprise the nucleus for our discussion of office automation in the chapters following.

The systems concept deals with the boundaries within which an analysis of paper work is conducted. It places emphasis upon the entirety, yet stresses the harmonious interrelationships of the parts making up that entirety. Using a systems concept, the analyst tackles the big picture, or the whole, but he is also concerned with how the parts of that picture mesh together into a harmonious unity. The systems concept frees the analyst from the approach of concentrating his efforts upon a single component and successively analyzing each component separately until all the components, or the entirety, are studied. The systems concept is actually not new, but it has gained prominence in the new office technology. The development of the systems concept is a natural outgrowth of having equipment available which can unify office operations among departments, distribute information between widely separated locations, and interrelate data-processing efforts among the traditionally functional divisions of an enterprise. The systems concept supplies the mental medium to conceive and utilize large portions of information projects, which portions are in keeping with the capacities of the physical equipment to be used in processing and handling this information.

Among the initial efforts to improve the processing of data was the idea to put source data into a form so that they could be reused as needed without the necessity of rewriting the source data each time they were to be used. Further, if this form could be made common to all the standard machines of an office, it would be possible to process the data utilizing the type of machine needed without having to rewrite or reenter the information for each machine. Also, the processing of data could be integrated. To illustrate, the punched card into which the data are captured by means of punched holes is a widely known example of a medium which facilitates source data automation. Once the data are captured in the card, they can be processed by a variety of equipment. Without doubt the accomplishment of keeping data in a form reusable between processing steps is one of the outstanding hallmarks in the area of the new office technology.

Third, the electronics technology is so significant that many feel it is synonymous with office technology. The computer is king and the center about which much office automation revolves. What has been accomplished with it staggers the imagination, but even more exciting is to dream what new uses may be made of computers and to strive to discover and ultimately to perfect such disclosures. The computer is without peer as a catalyst for new ideas. It is not just another office tool but a giant marvel awaiting our command. We must, however, know or learn how to direct this force in an effective manner. Computers, while accounting for the biggest share of electronics technology—and in which we are here most interested—are only a portion of the whole story. Automatic control arrangements which unite manufacturing control with data collecting and processing, and communications devices and communications switching devices are also a part of this technological change.

Each of these three major headings or structural members—the systems concept, source data automation, and the electronics technology— has been advanced by tremendous progress in equipment design and availability. Also each has fostered the growth of the other two. These observations are logical because the three developments themselves are outgrowths of a technology—in this case the office technology. And they are interrelated because they come from and have developed within a common major movement—again, the office technology.

CHAPTER TWO

AUTOMATION AND THE SYSTEMS AND PROCEDURES APPROACH

*Doing is the great thing. For if, resolutely, people do
what is right, in time they come to like doing it.*
—John Ruskin

OFFICE work is being revolutionized by the systems and procedures approach. We are hearing more about "systems," and managers are placing increasing emphasis on systems to meet the need for fast and accurate information and to make effective use of modern technological facilities for processing data. Systems are having a fundamental and broad-based impact upon all functions of an enterprise. Proven techniques, skills, and practices of the systems and procedures approach have been developed to produce meaningful time-saving results. In this and the following chapter we shall discuss the essentials of systems so that a basic comprehension of them is gained and their importance in the current office technology is realized.

EXISTENCE OF SYSTEMS

There is nothing new about the concept of systems. It is as old as mankind. Early in life we become acquainted with the solar system and later discover that we ourselves have digestive, nervous, and circulatory systems. In business, reference is commonly made to the inventory control system, the marketing system, the financing system, and so forth. Systems have been with us for many years.

For convenience, systems can be classified in any of several ways. The classifications of *physical* systems and *abstract* systems sometimes are

21

helpful. The former includes the human digestive system and the blood circulatory system, for example, while the latter would include the purchasing system and the shipping system of an enterprise. Classifications of similar meaning but with different names are *natural* systems and *man-made* systems. These terms are self-explanatory. Natural systems are those of physical or organic origin; they evolve from sources beyond the control of man, or nearly so. In contrast, man-made systems are designed by man to bring about a desired result by modifying or constraining performance, development, or action of selected basic resources.

SYSTEM IDENTIFIED

In many instances, an ordinary activity, commonly viewed as a single activity, is in reality made up of many different and relatively less important activities. Upon close examination we recognize the existence of an orderly relationship of some sort among these various lesser activities making up the entirety. And we discover that the interaction among the lesser actions or parts is necessary so that the entirety or end product performed is in keeping with accomplishing a given goal. Systems-minded people have been viewing problems in this light for many years.

Figure 4 illustrates graphically an activity common in business and

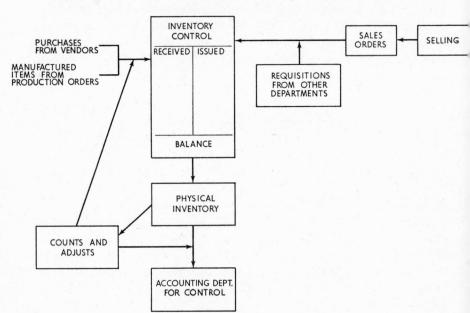

FIG. 4.   A system of inventory control.

one familiar to most of us. It shows the various activities making up a system of inventory control. In other words to insure adequate amounts of the right types of materials being on hand, we follow a man-made system designed to accomplish our objective. Various activities are coordinated in this effort. As indicated in the upper left of the figure, parts are either purchased from outside suppliers or we make them ourselves. These receipts are balanced with what we need, as revealed by sales orders and requisitions from other departments. Shipment of sales orders are made from storeroom supply. A level of inventory is maintained to permit taking care of the sales orders in this manner. In addition, control of physical counts and the supplying of data to the accounting department are included in the system.

This all appears simple enough, but we must note that a single entry on this chart, such as "purchases from vendors," entails a whole series of actions. From whom is a certain purchase made, when, what papers are used, what information is used to confirm purchase price, and so forth are the types of action involved. We use a term to identify such a sequence of operations for achieving a definite type of informational work. It is office procedure.

We will discuss office procedures more, but for the present we can say that the system shown in Figure 4 consists of and ties together three office procedures. Specifically this illustrated system of inventory control is made up of (1) the procedure for purchasing from vendors or from ourselves, (2) the procedure for issuing for sales orders which are shipped from the storeroom supply, and (3) the procedure for determining the physical inventory on hand.

We are now ready to define system. *It is a network of procedures which are integrated and designed to carry out a major activity.* We can think of a system as providing an orderly relationship among the parts and the whole. The large overall picture is included, yet the interrelations of the various parts making up this large picture are each given their proper attention both within the part itself and in its relation to the entirety. That is, the efficiency of each part, as well as the concern for the overall performance of the whole, is retained. In effect, the systems approach brings integration of related activities into the picture. Information which used to be considered and handled as separate entities is brought together. Fragmentation of information is minimized. Highlighted is the composite end result of many different informational activities working in many different ways. We consider the components as a dynamic totality or interaction of parts which is more important than the components themselves.

THE SYSTEMS VIEWPOINT

From the office management viewpoint, a system can be looked upon as a vehicle of thought and analysis. It is an attitude or way of viewing projects and problems in office management. A system has been called a "think process tool." This identity stresses system as providing the medium of thought and it implies utilization of an encompassing approach, yet retention of and regard for the components making up the entirety employed.

The use of systems in office management stresses conceptual skills of the manager. He must be able to visualize and understand the relationships between the information management job and all functions of the enterprise. For example, he must be able to gain a vivid mental picture of the effect of a change in materials control activity in a plant or in the sales order handling activity. Likewise, the ability to determine the effect of a new production control plan on the current cost control activity must be present.

EXTENSIVENESS AND INTEGRATION OF INFORMATION FLOW

From what has been stated it follows that the system concept can be applied to many facets of office management. As already indicated (Chapter 1) we can view an entire business enterprise as a system. In this case there are various component activities—producing, selling, financing, and so forth—which, in operation together, make up the entirety. In the same manner, production control, marketing research, handling accounts receivable, and so forth, can be viewed as systems, although in these cases the entirety, or scope of work, included is more limited than that where the entire business enterprise is considered as the system.

The extensiveness and the integration of the information flow arising from various activities are important. Firmly realizing these basic characteristics assists in grasping the fundamental concept of what makes up a system and employing it advantageously in office management work. To demonstrate further the relationships that exist, Figure 5 is included. This illustrates vividly the multitude of different, yet integrated, activities involved in receiving, manufacturing, and shipping customers' orders. Production requirements, for example, necessitate parts, labor, a manufacturing program, and facilities planning. Parts are either purchased from vendors or manufactured. If purchased, as shown in the figure, a number of activities are performed, including selecting the vendors, negotiating terms of purchase, following up purchase orders, receiving parts, having

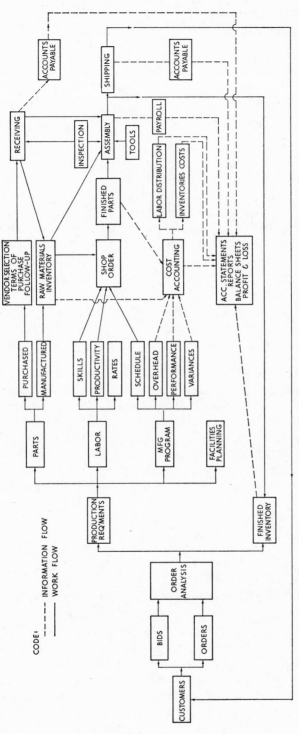

FIG. 5. The receiving, manufacturing, and shipping of customers' orders give rise to an extensive informational flow which is integrated by means of office systems.

them inspected, sending either to raw materials inventory or to assembly, and reporting receipts so that accounts payable can be made. The figure is indicative, but not conclusive. The task of systems integration is never simple. The overall framework is first conceived and then each informational segment, required by certain people to perform their specific work, is fitted into this entirety. Relating each segment to the overall pattern, or system, is vital.

SYSTEMS AND OFFICE TECHNOLOGY

Despite the complexity of business, the use of systems was limited until the availability of automated ways of processing data. As the source data automation technique became more widely known and computers became available, managers began to recognize the merit of using the systems concept. A number of the initial automated installations dealt with single isolated activities. Soon it was discovered that either needless duplication existed or certain voids in information were present, especially in relation to isolated activities. Furthermore, the scope of the automated processes and the quantity of data which could be handled within a short period suggested that a broader viewpoint or a larger scope of work be undertaken. In other words, man's concept of what could be accomplished had to be broadened in order to take advantage of the technical advances in data processing.

The systems concept is part of man's need and desire to sharpen his conceptual tools for solving his informational problems. Computers alone, with their capacity, versatility, and speed, cannot supply the answers. What they do is enable man to solve informational problems that heretofore were beyond his scope. Now he has the technical means available, but to utilize them, he must upgrade his conceptual horizons, identify critical informational problems, conceive the solutions to these problems, and evaluate their potential gain. This is a human prerogative and constitutes a vital challenge to modern office managers.

SYSTEMS, PROCEDURES, METHODS

We stated above that included in the makeup of a system is a network of procedures. Or stated differently, the coordination of related procedures can be thought of as making up a system. Hence, procedures are always included in a system. The term "systems and procedures" is in common usage. It gives recognition to both systems and procedures, but frequently the terminology of either "systems" or "procedures" may be employed. Systems would normally include systems and procedures, whereas procedures may be inclusive of procedures only, although in some instances the concept of systems is also implied.

The term "subsystem" is also used in discussions of systems. A subsystem is an integral part of a system and consists of two or more related procedures. The term, subsystem, is always subordinate to and used in reference to a system. For certain purposes of analysis, the concept of a system and its subsystems is helpful. Considered in and of themselves several related procedures are not referred to as making up a subsystem; they make up a system. To qualify as a subsystem the viewpoint must encompass or imply that the subsystem is subordinate to the system.

Procedures are of special interest in the management of office work. An "office procedure" can be defined as *a series of related clerical steps, usually performed by more than one person, which constitute an established and accepted way of carrying on an entire major phase of office activity*. Procedures are obtained by preplanning the various steps believed necessary to accomplish the work. Procedures are applied to the handling of such things as incoming orders, accounts payable, purchase orders, making up payrolls, sending out statements, and handling mail. An office procedure is broad in scope, frequently extending throughout a large portion of the entire office.

For clarity we will also define methods at this time. The term "method" designates *the manner of work performance of a task consisting of one or more clerical acts by an individual employee*. To a degree, methods become quite routine under an automated arrangement. Methods planning is more important when manual means are followed. A series of methods which are cumulative and integrated make up a procedure. And, to repeat, several procedures which are related and integrated make up a system.

In other words, as we successively narrow our scope of thinking about the manner of work performance, we utilize the concepts of systems, procedures, and methods. It is logical to determine first the system, then the procedures making up this system, and finally the methods making up each procedure. In this way the broad activities are established, coordination is enhanced, the feasibility of automation effectively determined, and the end result of the total effort is clearly visualized. In practice, however, the office planner or analyst gives some consideration to procedures and methods while designing the system and to methods while designing the procedure. This is taking the bottom-to-top viewpoint and this is usually helpful in connection with the top-down viewpoint. The latter viewpoint, however, is dominant. To reverse this approach by starting with methods, tying them together for the procedure, and tying procedures together for the system, is possible, but usually results in coordination difficulties and in excessive work scopes covered by the procedures and the systems.

SYSTEMS AND PROCEDURES IN OFFICE MANAGEMENT

For many years managers utilized the "look-see" practice in managing their enterprises. By this means the manager had his group working close at hand, gave orders directly to them, and exercised his managerial influences mainly by watching what the members of the group were doing. This overseeing characteristic of management was universal.

In modern business, the "look-see" management is rapidly diminishing. Mainly because of human complexity, size, and number of work specialties, today's manager can no longer look, see, and know the work results. He must use information as an indirect substitute for the "look-see" technique. Simply strolling by the desks and files to see how things are going, or talking with a few supervisors or group leaders, really doesn't provide much information of any value. The sample is insignificant and certain important criteria are not visible. The modern manager needs (1) a system which provides him accurate information as a substitute for the "look-see" approach and (2) an ability to interpret and understand the real significance of this information. The information is the type needed to help him perform his fundamental managerial functions, namely, his planning, controlling, organizing, and actuating efforts.

Much of today's office work—much in fact of *all* work—is accomplished through systems and procedures rather than by means of direct orders guided by what is obtained from the "look-see" approach. "Management by information" is a term that can be used to describe this new look. The trend in this direction is noticeable. For example, a manager doesn't have to be on the site of his operations. Information centers where decision making takes place are becoming common. All indications point to the increasing importance of management by information and the decreasing use of "look-see" management.

In this change, the emphasis upon systems and procedures in office management is apparent. They are fundamental in obtaining, processing, and distributing information to those who use it and in a form and at a time and place that they need it. Systems and procedures are, indeed, the basis for a completely harmonious and orderly operation of office work. More than this, the success or failure of most enterprises today depend in great measure on how carefully the office systems and procedures are developed and how well they are controlled in expediting the flow of information into and out of the enterprise.

Systems and procedures handle cycles of business activity, that is, they identify and establish sequences of specific activities for achieving definite types of office work. Referring to Figure 4 again, this system includes three specific procedures. If well planned this system will establish these procedures as essential to achieve the goal desired, coordinate them, prescribe the precise methods making up each procedure, and synchronize the methods within each procedure. Thus, an effective unity is derived from the various components, and this unity moves efficiently toward accomplishing the stated objective.

A challenge of the manager of information is to determine what systems and combinations of office procedures and methods is best for a given enterprise. The complexity of modern information handling negates the approach of considering each information requirement as a separate, isolated, and independent entity. The office manager cannot plan piecemeal and add parts together, taking a paper here, a machine there, a tape from still another area, and hope they all will fit together, work right, and give agreeable results. Today, he must start with the objective and work backward, by asking how best this goal can be reached by the use of those facilities available to him or those that can be made available to him. The systems and procedures approach helps tremendously in these efforts.

ADVANTAGES OF SYSTEMS AND PROCEDURES

The importance of systems and procedures to improved office information management is brought out in clear relief by listing their outstanding advantages. Such a list:

1. *Supplies a realistic look at an enterprise.* There is little question that in the final analysis an enterprise is an entirety. It exists to fulfill definite overall objectives. Each of its parts, departments, or units, no matter how compartmentized, contributes, as a result of the total, to the overall objectives. By adopting the systems and procedures approach it is possible to comprehend the entirety yet appreciate the operation of the various parts, separately and as a group, in achieving a particular goal.

2. *Increases appreciation for the total problem.* The broad and sweeping scope of systems and procedures enables a manager to see the total problem with its ramifications of various degrees of intensity in different areas of the enterprise. His thinking is focused on concern for the entirety with due regard for each part making up that entirety. What is under study is clearly delineated. In the very real meaning of the word, the relative importance of problems can be ascertained. Systems and procedures cut a swath through limited, departmentized, outmoded, and cobwebbed notions.

3. *Identifies the ingredients and the output.* It is always helpful to know what is required and what is obtained from any given activity. With the input and output highlighted, an evaluation of the type of data

required in order to get certain other derived data can prove helpful in that the feasibility of the work and whether it appears worthwhile can be readily determined.

4. *Brings order and a desirable mode of operation to office work.* Systems and procedures reduce everyday work to a routine, simplifying the execution of the work and minimizing the task of decision making in the handling of that work. Thus, management members are relieved of many details of execution, making it possible for them to devote most of their time to other work. The carrying out of the usual and frequent tasks is taken care of by the systems and procedures. Thus, only the out-of-the-ordinary or exceptional matters are referred to the executive, who decides what is to be done in these cases. This practice is referred to as the "exception principle" in management literature.

5. *Gives uniformity of actions and formalizes the work.* Common clerical tasks are handled in an identical manner each time they occur. Work can be easily located and quick checks on progress can be made. Well-designed paper forms, work habits, and controls can be utilized. In effect, systems formalize the related procedures, and procedures formalize the successive clerical steps so that an omission of any one of them is unusual. Thus, the chances of error are reduced. Furthermore, the possibility of any inaccuracy in the work at any one point is minimized, since an employee becomes particularly efficient and adept at his operation because of specialization and repetition.

6. *Emphasizes accurate and reliable controls.* Systems and procedures show the existence or not of checks and mechanisms whose purpose is to maintain accuracy, reliability, or other types of controls over the data. The overall picture utilized makes it possible to employ only those controls necessary for the whole system, thus lowering costs while retaining needed control over the work. Also, it can be arranged that the development of nonacceptable output triggers corrective action so that the work is kept within the provisions planned for it.

7. *Isolates and identifies problem areas.* The inclusive nature of systems and procedures makes it possible to spot problem areas quickly and accurately. Viewing the entire "work package" as a unit reveals the weak or trouble spots in their true relationship. Whereas an analysis of segment after segment may show no cause for alarm, an examination of the totality will reveal the difficulty. Some errors are magnified, others compensated for or neutralized by the total action and it is this type of helpful information which the systems and procedures approach supplies.

8. *Encourages application of management to broad concepts.* By the systems and procedures approach, uniform management practices are encouraged, thus contributing to an orderly and effective manner of per-

forming the work. Reliance upon rule-of-thumb measures and traditional modes of operation are minimized. Desirable results include greater efficiency, better coordination, a minimum of duplicated efforts and papers, and a more tightly knit and uniform work group.

9. *Facilitates automation of data processing.* Integrated data processing and the computer provide the practical means for handling large volumes of complicated data which apply to and cut across either small or large portions of an enterprise, the entire enterprise, or even the entire enterprise and outside influences. With the physical means available to process such data it is mandatory to have a medium facilitating the conceptualization of how the data might be processed to satisfy definite needs. Systems and procedures supply such a medium.

10. *Simplifies office personnel training.* The duties and operations of each job are clearly defined. Information is determined regarding what the employee must be capable of doing to perform the work satisfactorily. Selective training programs can be focused on the particular requirements needed by the employee.

11. *Improves the services of the office.* It is by means of procedures that the modern office is able to meet the large demands placed upon it. Getting the work out on time and in an acceptable form is possible through the help of office procedures. They make it possible to render the type of office service desired.

12. *Brings savings in the supplying of necessary information.* The work is kept moving, delay is minimized, employees are guided in their respective tasks, and unnecessary steps are eliminated.

SYSTEMS AND DATA PROCESSING

The requirements of the system, expressed in written and chart form, are transferred into specific processing activities in order for implementation to take place. In the case of manually or nonautomated processing, this transfer poses no new techniques. It is simply a matter of studying the map or guides and instructions precisely. The identity, sequence, and relationship of the operations are the base requirements. To a degree the same situation exists when source data automation is used. The means and locations for the source data are carefully determined and implemented. The various machines required are secured or made adaptable for the system requirements. The new manner of performing the work is then initiated and periodic follow-ups are made to insure that the processing is satisfactory.

However, when the processing is by computer we encounter a different situation. The system requirements must be transferred into a form which the computer can handle. Specifically, the relationship is between the system design and the computer programming function. What is computer programming? This is answered fully in Chapter 7, but for the present it will suffice to state that computer programming is a detail of the work in the form of a package of instructions for a computer to follow in order to process the work electronically.

To get from the system design to the computer program, a program flow chart and a block dia-

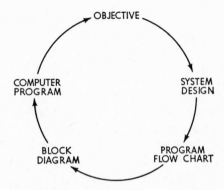

FIG. 6. Steps between objective statements and attainments when computer processing is employed.

gram are used. Figure 6 shows the arrangement. An objective is to be accomplished. To this end, a system is designed. The system is expressed in a program flow chart which, in turn, is expressed in the block diagram and computer program.

The program flow chart and block diagram show a detailed breakdown of the step-by-step activity requirements of the system. The extent to which the detail is carried depends upon the complexity and purpose of the work being processed. In some instances extreme details are in order while in other cases "reasonable" details suffice. When necessary details are missing, uncertainty, controversy, and needless discussions result. To illustrate the degree of detail, let us assume the system deals with payroll processing and we have progressed through steps (1) gross pay from straight salary, (2) gross pay from hourly rate, and (3) gross pay from incentive. The next steps are (4) develop deductions, and (5) get new up-to-date balance. Is step No. 4 in sufficient detail? To process it, we must (4.1) determine withholding tax, (4.2) determine F.I.C.A., and (4.3) calculate other approved deductions, i.e., for group insurance, union dues, and purchase of U.S. bonds. Unless these details are inserted in the computer program, the processing will fail. Carried further, we can ask, "Is step No. 4.1, 'determine withholding tax,' in sufficient detail?" Again the answer may be, "No," in which event either the block diagram should include the details or they must be added to the computer program. For step No. 4.1, additional details such as (4.11) exemption amount, (4.12) tax class, (4.13) existence of taxable income, and (4.14) tax amount might be needed.

Symbols are used in the preparation of program flow charts. Widely adopted and recommended symbols and their description are shown in Figure 7.

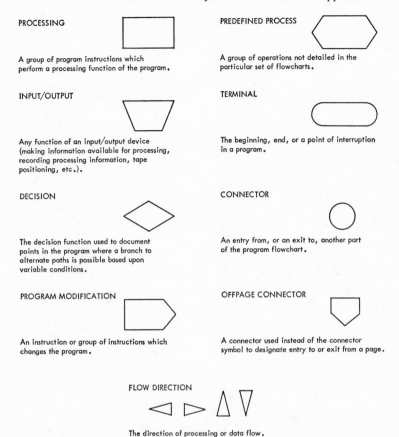

PROCESSING

A group of program instructions which perform a processing function of the program.

PREDEFINED PROCESS

A group of operations not detailed in the particular set of flowcharts.

INPUT/OUTPUT

Any function of an input/output device (making information available for processing, recording processing information, tape positioning, etc.).

TERMINAL

The beginning, end, or a point of interruption in a program.

DECISION

The decision function used to document points in the program where a branch to alternate paths is possible based upon variable conditions.

CONNECTOR

An entry from, or an exit to, another part of the program flowchart.

PROGRAM MODIFICATION

An instruction or group of instructions which changes the program.

OFFPAGE CONNECTOR

A connector used instead of the connector symbol to designate entry to or exit from a page.

FLOW DIRECTION

The direction of processing or data flow.

Courtesy: *International Business Machines Corp., White Plains, N.Y.*

FIG. 7. Program flow chart symbols and their descriptions.

In actual practice the systems man can stop at the system design and let the computer programmer develop from the system the block diagram and the computer program. In contrast, the systems man may extend his efforts all the way through computer programming, and turn over the complete package to the computer operator. Neither of these extremes is recommended. The best arrangement is an overlap in efforts in the area of reasonable details of the block diagram. In this way the systems man gains an understanding of programming and the programmer gains an understanding of the system design work. By developing jointly the graphic documents between system design and computer program, interfunctional cooperation increases, ambiguity of data is minimized, training is facilitated, and interdepartmental flexibility is encouraged.

Figure 8 shows the program flow chart for the application of calculating thermal differential means and variances. Beginning in the upper left, the first step is to test if switch B is on. If "Yes," indicated by letter "Y," the next step is to the right; if "No," indicated by letter "N," the next step is downward to Test C, to see if switch C is on. The successive steps progress downward in the left column of the figure to the bottom where point A is reached and continue in the column to the right.

From this program flow chart, the block diagram is developed. The start of this is shown by Figure 9. Block A is the start and consists of "Test if switch B is on." Moving to the right, block B is the next step, consisting of Test C, which is composed of "Test if switch C is on." Progressing to the right, the next step is indicated in Block C. To the right of each block are two columns for insertion of data needed for conversion to the computer. In block A, for example, in the first column are Y and N standing for "Yes" and "No." In the second column and opposite Y is 2L, meaning if the answer is "Yes," the successive step is 2L; in the same column opposite N is B, meaning if the answer is "No," the successive step is B, or block B, shown to the right of block A. The meaning of 2L is a code for a program modification which in this case is "set time switch to transfer setting" as indicated in Figure 8, upper left, as the step following a "Yes" answer to the question, "Is switch B on?" By studying Figure 8 in conjunction with the block diagram of Figure 9, the identity and need for each block of Figure 9 is revealed, along with the coded operations which the computer must perform.

BASIC OBSERVATIONS ABOUT SYSTEMS

Systems are valuable, for they are the means by which related activities are integrated. The effective flow of information, by which each individual employee or organization unit receives proper information in order to perform its work better, is expedited by systems. There are, however, questions regarding what information is proper and needed. To a degree systems can help answer these questions, but the basic problem is to determine for each unit, its goals and the information it needs to utilize management in reaching these goals.

It is important to point out that each unit not only receives information to guide it, but it also produces information of importance to others. That is, there is a receiving and a giving of information by each unit. This can be identified as "input-output" and applies either to one or to a totality made up of a number of units. This input-output characteristic makes for a chain of information which expedites system design. It also makes realistic the expression "flow of information."

Within their defined boundaries, systems are all-inclusive. They cut across common compartmentations recognized by organization, custom, and personal preferences. All essential component activities, regardless of their location or degree of contribution, are taken into account by a system. The guiding rule is to encompass all informational needs and contributions bearing on the objective of the system.

Systems are made up of multitudinous interrelated parts which comprise still further interrelated parts, and, in turn, still further interrelated parts. Within an office system, for example, there are coordinated office procedures, and within an office procedure, coordinated methods. They are all, or should be, closely knit together.

Every system has a feedback of information which gives actual results being obtained. This characteristic follows naturally because a system is an entity within itself designed to accomplish certain work. The revealing of the degree to which this work is over- or underachieved is a natural outgrowth of the system's inherent properties.

WHO DESIGNS SYSTEMS AND PROCEDURES?

From what has been stated in this chapter, it follows that many, many tasks must be performed by a systems and procedures man and this requires considerable competency. With the increasing emphasis in this area, specialists in systems work have developed. They are termed systems and procedures men or sometimes the names "systems men," "systems engineers," or "systems analysts" are used. Illustrative of what can be considered typically the basic functions and duties of a systems designer is shown by Figure 10 (page 38).

High on the list of desirable qualifications is conceptual ability, along with imagination and objectivity. He must be able to see future possibilities in untried systems and procedures and anticipate possible trouble areas. Also, the ability to initiate and "dream practical dreams" are genuine assets. In addition, it is helpful to possess a general yet fundamental grasp of the background activities within which the system is designed and operated. The systems designer must constantly update his knowledge of techniques, tools, and equipment. New and better ways are constantly appearing in this special area. Definitely advantageous to the systems and procedures man are mental alertness and curiosity and an understanding of human nature. He must have the ability to work in harmony with top managers, to sympathize with them, and understand their problems, and to push forward in his efforts despite complaints and disappointments. Finally, the art and skill of communication must be developed, for the systems and procedures man must be able to share his ideas, findings, and suggestions clearly and concisely.

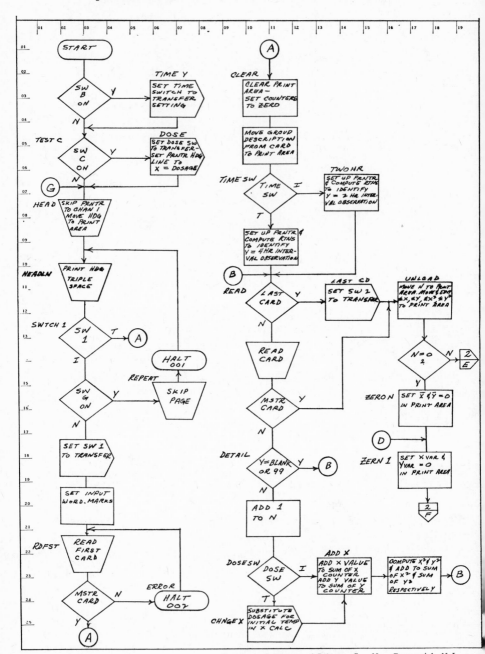

FIG. 8.   A program flow chart.

START — EST IF WITCH B S ON Y 2L / N B	**B TESTC** — TEST IF SWITCH C IS ON Y 2M / N C	**C HEAD** — SKIP PRINTER TO CHANNEL 1 AND MOVE HEADING TO PRINTER OUTPUT AREA	**D HEADLN** — PRINT HEADING + TRIPLE SPACE	**E SWITCH 1** — LOGIC SWITCH 1 I F / T K
SST IF WITCH G S ON Y 2F / N G	**G** — SET SWITCH 1 TO TRANSFER SETTING	**H** — SET INPUT WORD MARKS	**J RDFST** — READ FIRST CARD + TEST IF MASTER CARD Y K / N 2G	**K CLEAR** — CLEAR PRINT AREA + SET COUNTERS TO ZERO MOVE GROUP DESCR. FROM CARD TO PRINTER AREA
TIMESW — LOGIC SWITCH TIME I 2H / T M	**M** — SET UP PRINTER + COMPUTE ROUTINES TO IDENTIFY Y = 4 HOUR INTERVAL OBSERVATION	**N READ** — TEST IF LAST CARD READ Y U / N O	**O** — READ CARD + TEST IF MASTER CARD Y V / N P	**P DETAIL** — TEST IF Y VALUE IS BLANK OR 99 Y N / N Q
ADD 1 TO N	**R DOSESW** — LOGIC SWITCH DOSE I S / T 2N	**S ADD X** — ADD X VALUE TO SUM OF X COUNTER ADD Y VALUE TO TO SUM OF Y COUNTER	**T** — COMPUTE X^2 AND Y^2 AND ADD TO SUM OF X^2 AND SUM OF Y^2 RESPECTIVELY N	**U LASTCD** — SET SWITCH 2 TO TRANSFER SETTING
UNLOAD — VE N TO PRINT EA. MOVE+EDIT $\bar{X}, \Sigma Y, \Sigma X^2 + \Sigma Y^2$ O PRINT AREA	**W** — TEST IF N = 0 Y 2J / N X	**X** — COMPUTE $\bar{X} = \frac{\Sigma X}{N}$ + $\bar{Y} = \frac{\Sigma Y}{N}$ + MOVE TO PRINT AREA	**Y** — SUBTRACT 1 FROM N AND TEST IF =0 Y 2K / N Z	**Z** — COMPUTE X + Y VARIANCES + MOVE TO PRINT AREA $X_{VAR} = \dfrac{\Sigma X^2 - \frac{(\Sigma X)^2}{N}}{N-1}$
PRINT — RINT LINE + DOUBLE SPACE	**B SWITCH2** — LOGIC SWITCH 2 I C / T D	**C** — TEST IF PAGE OVERFLOW Y 1C / N 1K	**D END JOB** — SKIP TWO PAGES AND HALT 000, 999	**E** — SET SWITCHES 1+2 AND DOSE + TIME SWITCHS TO N. TIAL SETTING SET PRINTER HEADING LINE TO X=TEMP. 1A
REPEAT — SKIP PAGE AND HALT 000,001 1D	**G ERROR** — HALT 000,002 1J	**H TWCHR** — SET UP PRINTER + COMPUTE ROUTINES TO IDENTIFY Y = 2 HOUR INTERVAL OBSERVATION 1N	**J ZERON** — SET $\bar{X} + \bar{Y} = C$ IN PRINT AREA	**K ZERN 1** — SET $X_{VAR} + Y_{VAR} = 0$ IN PRINT AREA A
TIME 4 — ET TIME WITCH TO RANSFER SETTING 1B	**M DOSE** — SET DOSE SWITCH TO TRANSFER SETTING + SET PRINTER HEADING LINE TO X=DOSAGE 1C	**N CHNGE X** — SUBSTITUTE DOSAGE FOR INITIAL TEMPERATURE IN X CALCULATIONS 1S	**O**	**P**
	R	**S**	**T**	**U**
	W	**X**	**Y**	**Z**

FIG. 9. A block diagram for conversion work to computer.

Title: Analyst—Systems and Procedures   Div: Allen Plant
Dept.:   Staff   Job No.:   33

Basic Functions:

Plans, develops, recommends, implements, and coordinates the systems and procedures activities within the Allen Plant. Advises vice-president in charge of this plant on matters of systems and procedures to promote administrative efficiency and reduce clerical costs.

Duties:

Within the authority limits authorized by divisional policies, he has the following duties:

1. Advise and assist the vice-president in regard to proposed systems and procedures.
2. Develop, recommend, and establish an effective cost and inventory system. This includes development of an effective manner for handling receipts and disbursements, handling vendors' and customers' claims, and taking and reporting physical inventories.
3. Review existing systems and procedures periodically in order to introduce improvements and controls to provide better service and lower cost.
4. Develop and maintain a Systems and Procedures Manual for the division to assure conformity to the pattern and format established by the corporation.
5. Coordinate the office mechanization program with all interested staff and operating personnel.

*   *   *   *   *

10. Keep informed on current developments in the area of systems and procedures, appraise their value for the division, and recommend adoption when advisable.

Approved   *James E. Elgin*
Authorized   *Henry Puterbaugh*
Date   *July 2, 196—*

FIG. 10.   A systems and procedures job description.

CHAPTER THREE

THE ULTIMATE—THE TOTAL SYSTEMS CONCEPT

Don't be afraid to take a big step if one is indicated.
You can't cross a chasm in two small jumps.
—David Lloyd George

THE USE of the systems and procedures approach has proven to be highly effective in defining an informational problem and in evolving the required solution. Further, the potential benefits of office automation are greatest when the systems and procedures approach provides the vehicle of analysis and design regarding what pattern of processing should be followed. In other words, we have progressed in utilizing technological improvements at least to some satisfactory degree by considering elements as a dynamic totality, by viewing this totality as being more important than its components, and by recognizing the interaction of the components as being highly significant. .

THE LOGICAL DEVELOPMENT

Better definition of the problem in its true setting and the extensiveness of systems and procedures led logically to the idea of extending the systems concept to include other related systems as a totality. Why stop with one system? Is not one system related to other systems so that an overall inclusive viewpoint of several systems is not only desirable but entirely practical?

Figure 11 shows a system for inventory control and sales. This was derived by adding to the system for inventory control (left portion of figure) the system for sales (right portion of figure). The former, or system for inventory control, was discussed in Chapter 2 and illustrated by Figure 4. Compared to that shown in Figure 4, the system shown in

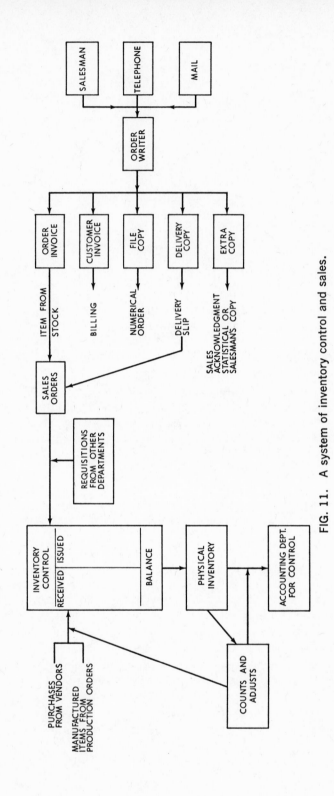

FIG. 11. A system of inventory control and sales.

Figure 11 is more comprehensive, more meaningful, and more expeditious for utilizing modern office automation equipment. It shows a "bigger picture," the interaction of activities and a greater volume of related work which can be considered in deciding the processing means.

Thus, moving from a single system idea to that of several systems as the vehicle of thought in informational efforts, was a logical development. From the historical viewpoint this was a natural outgrowth. During the early periods of work study, attention was focused on the task of an individual and how it was performed. Expanding this concept the related tasks of several individuals were considered, resulting in the development of a procedure. Later, related procedures were considered and the concept of a system became accepted. Continuing, from considering several related systems evolved the idea of a project, and from many related systems, the idea of an entire enterprise.

Furthermore, during the past few decades there has been a trend to integrated control in which the entire production process from raw materials to finished products, along with all sales efforts, are consolidated. This same trend has led to mergers among enterprises of considerable size. These changes have given emphasis to the need for reliable information of what has gone on and what is proposed should go on, throughout the entire enterprise. In many cases information was far from integrated, and the natural tendency was to try to develop a consolidated information system that would effectively provide the facts that were needed.

Slowly but surely, it became recognized that information is crucially interdependent. What happens in one organizational unit influences what happens in other organizational units. No one bit of information is an island unto itself. It is related to and affects other bits of information. With this fundamental in mind, the natural development was toward a more inclusive and all-encompassing concept about data gathering and processing.

THE TOTAL SYSTEMS CONCEPT

What is meant by the total systems concept? The answer: The integration of necessary systems within an enterprise to provide timely information derived from rigorously determined relationships and needs of the enterprise. With the total systems concept, a reservoir of information would be available to any management member in the enterprise any time it is needed. The probable impact of any contemplated action in any one segment upon the entire enterprise could be easily and quickly ascertained. Purchasing, marketing, and engineering data could be readily combined with material control, inventory, quality, and production flow information. Research and development progress could be tied in with forecasting; thus where and when to make engineering changes in a product line could be accurately calculated. In brief, complete legal, historical, fiscal, and operational data would be included and interrelated.

A graphic representation indicating the general idea of a total systems concept is shown by Figure 12. This is suggestive only and is not intended to be conclusive. Beginning at the top of the figure, top management members, either as individual department heads or as a group, perform basic operations which establish objectives and supply the necessary parameters within which these objectives will be sought. These resulting decisions are forwarded to an Information Service Center which cuts across all organization lines, is centralized, reports to top management members, receives feedback information on actions taken, and regulates information flow. As depicted, the Information Service Center is able to provide top managers with the broad scope of analytical and control data available and in use, plus the information flow related to forecasts, actual performances, feedback, evaluation, and coordination. Thus, effective implementation of information is enhanced and adequate control over it is provided. More specifically, and as shown in the figure, the Information Service Center designs and installs systems, processes data, and supervises information flow. This is done to establish fundamental practices shown on the figure, practices such as stock review, raw materials control, work in process control, product cost reports, and payroll accounting and variance. Feedback is obtained on all these practices by determining for each case the exception to what is wanted (management by exception) and taking the needed corrective action. The automatic feedback is indicated at the bottom of the illustration.

As illustrated, and in most cases, the total systems concept is based on forecasts of requirements over reasonable periods, together with establishment of the optimum manufacturing and selling plans based on the forecast. What is optimum can be from a cost, service, time, or capability viewpoint. Furthermore, implied in the total systems concept are determinations for control limits within which the forecast will remain unchanged, feedbacks of actual requirements compared to the forecasts, and corrective actions either in the form of forecast adjustments or in operations. This is to say that manufacturing and selling efforts are based on the forecasts, not on actual requirements. The latter may vary sufficiently to suggest an adjustment in the forecast, and this is done when the forecast is obviously out of line. But fluctuations within established limits can occur without affecting the forecast.

The total systems concept is so logical that one wonders why we did not

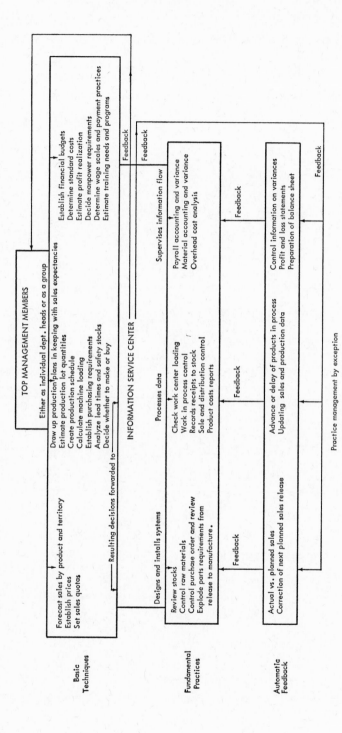

FIG. 12. A concept of total systems for an enterprise.

get to it sooner or why it is not universally adopted. Actually the reasons are many. During the initial adoption of office automation there was some tendency to automate the work that had always been done. The existent systems or procedures were given a sacred, do-not-alter status. Any new information needs were patched onto the old systems or procedures. Reports, records, data of all kinds were seldom culled, and if so, rarely in their entirety. Customarily any inspection was confined to a portion of the entirety. The result was that useless information was permitted to exist, even ignored, without purpose and without controls. In some instances the difficulty probably was in the location and status of the data-processing group. When they alone decide what information they will produce, when they will produce it, and for whom, the total systems concept may suffer. Even when department heads' requests for data are answered, the approach may be strictly departmental, rather than on an enterprise basis, for the department head is most likely to request data of interest to his department only. As a result, other uses for the data processed are not considered.

To facilitate the total systems concept requires three essential factors. First, information handling—including the acquiring, processing, and distributing—must be granted top status and top management attention and backing. The management members must have, or be developed to have, an appreciation for the total systems concept. Changes must be made for the total systems concept to be utilized. They must see information handling as an enterprise activity, not a departmentized or particular specialty for their own isolated use. Second, modifications and improvements of present systems are in order to reflect the completely integrated enterprise-wide total systems concept. Third, new, overall systems should be evolved, installed, and kept up to date. This constitutes a tremendous challenge and a lot of hard work, but it will bring many benefits to everyone in the entire enterprise.

IDENTIFYING CHARACTERISTICS

In order for the total systems concept to serve as a fundamental approach for guidance in all systems work, we must comprehend its identifying characteristics. To assist in this purpose, Figure 13 has been included. Starting at the top and moving clockwise, the circle represents the logical cycle, starting with objectives and eventually ending with objectives accomplished. Efforts to achieve the objectives are constrained by the enterprise's parameters such as contractual obligations, work force, and type of machines. In addition, boundaries are set by outside

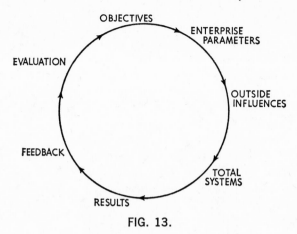

FIG. 13.

influences, i.e., those outside the enterprise's control, such as government regulations and trade practices. The efforts taken are guided and integrated by the provisions of the total systems, which can be said to govern the actions to be taken. The sequential work specified by the systems can be either manually or machine operated, subject to the cost and time evaluation involved in any specific circumstance. The work accomplishment brings about results indicated at the bottom of the illustration. The actions taken also supply the feedback essential for internal control. The provisions for the feedback are incorporated in the systems implemented in order to insure validity of the results. What is obtained, or the end of the performance, is subjected to evaluation in terms of its accomplishing the objectives as initially stated.

With this as a background, let us point out the essential characteristics of utilizing the total systems concept. First, and of great significance, is that objectives must be taken into consideration. They are the basis for determining both the formulation and the extent of the total systems utilized. Every individual system that is included in the total systems must be justified in terms of its contribution to the objectives. Second, related systems governing performance are integrated into logical total systems. Third, systems can and must be designed within the defined parameters of the enterprise and operative influences outside the enterprise. Lastly, the best means—usually mechanical or automatic—should be considered in the design and application of the systems followed in order that the work is performed most economically in keeping with the objectives and to the end that the right information is delivered to the right people, or where it has maximum value.

OBJECTIVES AND THE TOTAL SYSTEMS CONCEPT

Objectives are always important in management, but in discussing the total systems concept, objectives warrant special emphasis. What constitutes a system, or a total systems, is determined by the objectives sought. Thus the extent and number of systems we include in a total systems are dependent upon the objectives. An illustration commonly used to bring out this fact will be included here. Although the illustration deals with an automobile, it applies equally to information systems.

With reference to an automobile, the question can be asked, "What is an ignition system?" We would answer in terms something like the following. It is a system actually made up of a combination of several systems designed to make certain activities take place which result in sparks or electric flashes igniting combustible fuel. Note that identification of the several lesser systems is couched in terms of what the total systems are intended to achieve, or in terms of the objectives. We could go into the details of the lesser systems making up the total ignition system, such as the timing system, the condenser system, the spark plug system, and so forth, but this is irrelevant for the point at hand. Next, suppose the question is asked, "What are the total systems that deliver brake horsepower on the wheels of an automobile?" We would answer, the ignition system, the combustion system, the cooling and ventilating system, and the transmission system. All these systems work together to achieve the objective—deliver brake horsepower on the wheels of an automobile. Suppose we change our objectives to include the potential supplying of transportation to a human being. Since our objectives have changed, we change the inclusion of the systems making up the total systems. Specifically, we would add the system of steering, the system of braking, and a human being, with all the systems he brings with him, behind the steering wheel. Again, if our objectives were to include transporting this human being, we get into additional systems such as a system of roads, traffic lights, highway instructions, and so forth.

To reiterate, objectives establish the limits and utilization of the systems making up the total systems concept in any given case. In fact, the total systems concept is meaningful to the degree that the objectives are identified. Furthermore, this means that a total systems is not a grandiose composite of all systems to do all things. Rather, it is an integration of systems designed for the purpose of achieving stated objectives.

Too frequently the total systems idea is applied to objectives that are much too narrow. Existent data should be carefully scrutinized for its essentiality. New data can and should be generated to supply helpful data formerly unavailable or to reveal relationships that are helpful to know. In addition, objectives can include a magnitude that advances managerial effectiveness in that the total systems promote more penetrating thinking by management members, signal the appearance of sudden hazards or opportunities, along with the available alternatives of action to take about them, and highlight the key factors in common occurrences in enterprise.

ADVANTAGES OF TOTAL SYSTEMS CONCEPT

There are a number of advantages in the total systems concept. Some of these are fairly obvious, others not so evident. It will be helpful to point out these advantages. Foremost is the expediting of planning by means of systems. Planning dealing solely with a major segment of an enterprise may not fill the needs for a broad plan. In some instances, if a narrow scope is followed, it may even work counter to the interests of the enterprise as an entirety. However, when a particular system is planned as a part of a total systems for an enterprise, the system occupies a place compatible in the overall scheme of things and is properly related to the entirety. Also, an important advantage of the total systems concept is the feasibility of considering the impact of important decisions on all parts of an enterprise. It is therefore possible to reach decisions that will maximize profits of an enterprise as a whole, minimize costs of the enterprise as a whole, or to arrive at decisions which provide the most benefits to the enterprise, all parts of the enterprise being taken into account and given recognition in keeping with their respective contributions and value. In addition, the total systems concept makes feasible the utilization of present-day data-processing equipment, especially the highly efficient modern computer. One can reason that the computer served as a catalyst which stimulated thinking toward the total systems concept. Certainly the development of the total systems and the computer are intimately related. Being able to determine what data we want from the entire enterprise viewpoint, and being able to process and transmit these integrated data as needed, has made for a combination significantly important in office management. Improvements and new techniques in developing the total systems are continually being devised and along with them, new capacities and speeds of electronic equipment are being perfected.

Likewise, information is maintained in a single data stream by utilization of the total systems idea. This single vehicle for information serves all phases of the enterprise and normally insures greater accuracy and better format of the information, since decisions in all areas are based on this single uniformity of information flow. Confusion is minimized, standardization increased, and understanding expedited. Furthermore, day-to-day analyses or special studies can be provided. Total systems produce current information related to individual needs. The information is not confined to historical data or traditional reports and records. Neither is it delayed excessively by decision making at many levels and by noncoordinated and time-consuming clerical calculations. Another advantage, commonly overlooked, is that special analyses can be performed as a by-product of the total systems. Usually such analyses can be supplied with very little additional effort. Without total systems special analyses may be too costly or pose so many difficulties as to be considered impractical. Thus additional information helpful in arriving at better and more inclusive decisions is unavailable. Finally, mention of the type of problems solved, and at what cost, should be included. Complex, intricate problems that extend into every facet of the enterprise can be handled satisfactorily by the total systems approach. For by this approach, consideration is given to both the effect upon and contributions to possible solutions to problems of each segment of the enterprise as well as of the totality of the enterprise. The problems can be clearly identified and then related to the activities which they affect. And all this can be accomplished at a relatively low cost.

SHORTCOMINGS OF TOTAL SYSTEMS CONCEPT

We have already stated that top management attention and backing is one of the essential factors for success in the total systems concept. Actually this backing is not always present and, from a practical viewpoint, its absence constitutes one of the really serious shortcomings in utilizing total systems. How can one account for this situation? Part of the explanation may lie in the fact that most top executives reach the top by way of sales, production, or engineering. Relatively few come up through the accounting, personnel, or information areas. Hence, many have neither a full appreciation of the nature of information problems nor the means to cope with them. Also the area of information and all that goes with it—data, systems, procedures, processing, reports, and so forth —are not exciting subjects to top managers. They look upon a concept such as total systems as being helpful but not essential, useful but not exciting. The general attitude is that their efforts directed to other areas will pay bigger dividends.

The mere scope of total systems encourages numerous areas for specialization. It takes a very competent and informed man to be a good total systems designer and implementer. The tendency is to advocate the overall perspective but to emphasize and practice that about which one knows or thinks he knows the most, either by training or experience. As a result, specialization creeps in and the broad, balanced viewpoint falls by the wayside. A carefully evolved part—or parts—of the total systems is offered as the well-designed total systems, whereas it is only partially so. Furthermore, communication difficulties arise among the specialists. They have trouble conveying their exact needs and suggestions to each other. The total systems concept is evolved on what the meanings are believed to be rather than what they really are.

One of the most serious barriers to total systems, and in fact to all systems, is the temptation to cling to narrow approaches. The complete and full benefits of total systems can never be won by adhering to limited areas. For example, the need for a broad approach relates to the accounting system approach. The accounting system is certainly essential in enterprises today, yet it is not the sole occupant of a modern systems approach. Related to it and also of great significance are the production control system, the factory machine replacement system, and the credit and collections system. In addition, there is what is termed the mechanization, or automation, system which assumes that the only, or at least the best, means of improving office work performance is via a particular mechanized or automated route. For a given operation, time, and place, this may be true. As equipment is offered on the market, specialists to operate it develop. Usually their interest is mainly in processing the data. When further changes both in the enterprise's informational needs and in the equipment offered on the market take place, these mechanization people may actually represent an inflexibility element in updating the work to meet these current informational needs of the enterprise. To reiterate, the broad approach is necessary for the total systems concept to develop.

Another drawback to total systems progress and acceptance is the apparently persisting tendency to orientate systems efforts to specific problems as they arise. New systems are designed, or existing systems are revised, to bring about a solution to an immediate difficulty. The initial thinking is focused on patching up or repairing systems already in existence. If this can't be done, a new system is added to the existing old systems. True, service is stressed and this is commendable. But the long term effect of changes in present systems, and the occasional addition of a new one, is to emphasize isolated systems. Their interrelatedness is weakened. It should also be observed that the solving of one problem after another really does nothing to prevent other problems from arising and does not tackle the basic causes of their arising. Seldom followed is a fresh, new overall approach to determine what better systems in their totality might be used to improve the operations and the results.

Finally, there is the hidden characteristic of systems improvements.

Changes are not easily discerned and the benefits are intangible. The improvement in service or the reduction in cost is frequently neither as meaningful nor as evident as an increase in sales orders or a new production level attained by a factory force. Closely associated with this hidden characteristic is the desire for protection against possible blame should some part of the systems improvement not work out satisfactorily. This takes the form of extra copies, time stamps, initiating of memos, various checks, and logs. But these protective measures can far exceed in cost the delays or errors which they protect against, and they provide little help in determining the source of such delays or errors.

TOTAL SYSTEMS AND COST

The reduction of cost is commonly one of the reasons for utilizing total systems. Consideration for cost may be altered somewhat where other factors such as capability, time, service, or flexibility are accorded major significance. But cost is always in the picture. Capability, for example, may be traded down slightly in order to keep expenditures within a given amount. The objectives, established or expressed by what the users of the systems want or can be convinced to accept, have a strong influence on the ability to demonstrate savings or other advantages.

	System No. 1	System No. 2
One-Time Costs		
System studies	$ 10,000	$ 15,500
Conversion to new system	5,500	5,000
Test period	8,000	8,000
Miscellaneous expenses	2,500	1,500
Totals	$ 26,000	$ 30,000
Recurring Costs		
Processing equipment (rental)	$108,000	$137,000
Personnel		
System analysts	26,000	26,000
Operations	38,750	17,800
Supplies	22,500	14,000
Totals	$195,250	$194,800

FIG. 14.   Cost estimates for alternative systems.

In the case of a new system, the cost analysis should take into account *one-time costs,* or those incurred due to design and installation of a new system, and *recurring costs,* or those sustained to operate the new system installed. These concepts are brought out in Figure 14, which illustrates a cost comparison between two systems being considered. For system No. 1, the one-time costs consist of system studies, conversion to the new .system, a test period to insure satisfactory operation of system, and miscellaneous expenses. These total $26,000 as indicated in the figure. Comparable costs for system No. 2 are $30,000, shown on the right of the illustration. Recurring costs for system No. 1 include processing equipment rental, personnel, and supplies, and total $195,250. Comparable costs for system No. 2 are $194,800.

It is reasonable to prorate the one-time costs over five years. When this is done, we get $5,200 $\left(\dfrac{\$26,000}{5}\right)$ for system No. 1 and 6,000 $\left(\dfrac{\$30,000}{5}\right)$ for system No. 2. Adding the respective recurring costs for each system we get:

	System No. 1	System No. 2
Prorated one-time costs	$ 5,200	$ 6,000
Recurring costs	195,250	194,800
Totals	$200,450	$200,800

These respective totals are for each of the first five years. After that, the costs for each system would be the recurring costs only. This means that based on costs for the first five years, system No. 1 is more advantageous, while after five years, system No. 2 is. Specifically, by selecting system No. 2, costs would be $1,750 greater (5 × $350) but each year thereafter we would save some $450 ($195,250 − $194,800) by using system No. 2 in preference to system No. 1. At the end of nearly nine years from the beginning, we would have recouped the $1,750 disadvantage and go on to benefit by the $450 each year.

But is this the whole story? No. We should consider displaceable and nondisplaceable costs. The former are those that are removed with full implementation of the new system, the latter those that are not. Figure 15 shows the data taking into account these types of cost. The data are

	System No. 1	System No. 2
Up to Five Years		
One-time costs	$ 5,200	$ 6,000
Recurring costs	195,250	194,800
Nondisplaceable costs	122,500	122,500
Cost per year	$322,950	$323,300
Old system costs per year	323,000	323,000
New system savings per year	$ +50	$ −300
After Five Years		
Recurring costs	$195,250	$194,800
Nondisplaceable costs	122,500	122,500
Cost per year	$317,750	$317,300
Old system costs per year	323,000	323,000
New system savings per year	$+5,250	$+5,700

FIG. 15.

self-explanatory. With nondisplaceable costs of $122,500 and the old system cost of $323,000, for the first five years the cost advantage is in using system No. 1. However, after five years the advantage is with system No. 2. Again, we would select system No. 2 as the better system costwise over the long period.

However, the cost differential between these two systems is small and not very convincing. This would normally lead to giving intangibles considerable weight. Among these would be the relative evaluation of the two systems concerning flexibility, expansion possibilities, safety factor to meet load fluctuations, and preferences of knowledgeable employees. We might also investigate other costs, such as indirect costs of personnel, which in the illustration would probably be higher for system No. 1 since it requires more people as shown by the operations costs of $38,750 annually.

TOTAL INTEGRATED PERSONNEL SYSTEM

As is well known there is much record keeping in personnel. The work of recruiting, placing, transferring, promoting, counseling, training, and maintaining the traditional information about personnel involves considerable data handling. We should know, for example, each employee's work history, scores on tests, performance ratings, and general qualifications quickly so that the best job possible can be made of maintaining an effective and satisfied work force. What is needed is a way not only to handle personnel information more easily but also to free personnel staff people to do more constructive and creative work. How best can questions such as the following be answered. "What does it cost to recruit, train, and place a man?" "How many present employees have training and experience in operating a vertical boring machine? In conducting marketing research surveys? In public relations work?" "If the retirement age is reduced three years and base wages are raised 5 percent across the board, what will be the effect on wages and salaries and on the makeup of the work force?"

A Total Integrated Personnel System (TIPS) which is an automated personnel system, has been designed and installed in the Data Systems Division Laboratory of the International Business Machines Corporation in Poughkeepsie, N.Y.[1] By means of this system a complete resumé for each employee is developed and kept updated. An IBM 1410 computer is used. The data for each employee are printed under selected headings with the number of pages varying directly with the amount of data each

---

[1] The source of material for this discussion is: T. P. Byrnes and J. Correnti, "TIPS: A Total Integrated Personnel System," (Poughkeepsie, N.Y.: International Business Machines Corporation, May 20, 1964).

individual has. Basically the (1) personal data and (2) skills data are brought together in an automated central source from which information for each employee can be generated, including histories, skill searches, résumés, and the like.

Figure 16 shows the general arrangement followed from collecting data, centralizing them, and processing to provide information desired. Referring to the figure, data from the recruiting department are key punched and put into the computer, those from the education department are relayed to the personnel department from whence they are automated, likewise for information from the communications department and from the patent department. It required sound systems designing to provide a means for collecting all these data, preparing them for electronic processing, and providing the means for keeping the data updated by reporting changes and significant events as they occurred.

The end result is that complete information can be obtained quickly from one source. The data include:

Classification	Typical Inclusions
Personal	Name, address, birth date
Education	Course name, degree, scholastic honor
Past experience	Work, military service, patents
Activities	Professional groups, fraternal associations
Skills (several classified types)	Skill description, products worked on, foreign languages, preferences

The availability of this information, however, does not negate the need for competent personnel management members. It does eliminate much time-consuming routine searching and it identifies those meeting certain standards or criteria to fill a particular manpower need. Who is selected from an approved group remains the manager's decision. In other words, what TIPS provides is (1) a central source for all existing personnel data which are kept up to date, (2) a complete skills inventory to facilitate skills searches, selection of employees for retraining, and transferring of any employee available for reassignment, and (3) a source of classified information helpful in recruiting, manpower scheduling, and determining personnel development needs.

TOTAL SYSTEMS—A PRESENT EVALUATION

Observe that TIPS is really a total systems for the personnel department. It deals solely with personnel data. As such it is a limited version of the total systems concept but a highly successful accomplishment in that direction. But a short time ago the term "total systems," meaning totally integrated systems, was the rage. This was the utopia for

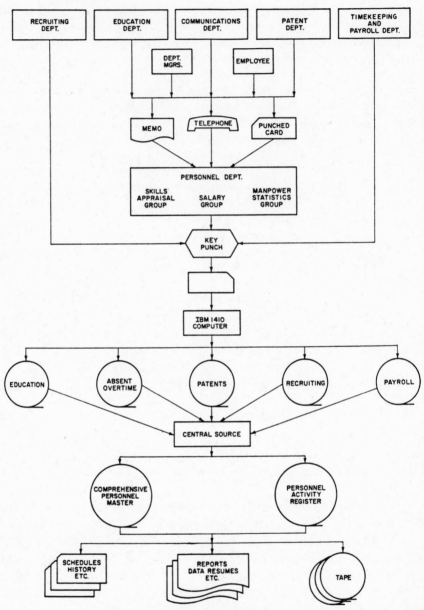

Courtesy: International Business Machines Corp., Poughkeepsie, N.Y.

FIG. 16.   A comprehensive personnel system.

information handling. Today much of the initial enthusiasm has been dispelled. However, this does not mean that the total systems concept is not valid. It would seem to suggest that the work involved in developing total systems for a given enterprise poses greater hurdles and is far more difficult and elusive than first suspected. Also, the complexity of the enterprise's operations, the competitive environment under which it operates, the urgency for a total systems, the caliber of systems men available, the attitude of top managers, and a host of additional factors are contributory. In the case of several large corporations manufacturing in many different locations and distributing nationally and internationally, encompassing relationships with a multitude of vendors, customers, employees, communities, shareowners, and governments, the thought has been advanced that the total systems concept is too broad and too large to use effectively. It is claimed that satisfactory results, at least for the present, are possible with something less than total systems.

The present status is one of degree more than of kind. If total systems cannot be used, some degree of it can. There is unanimity of opinion that within an enterprise a partial total systems is superior to several large but noncoordinated systems. As pointed out above, we specify the extensiveness of the coordination by the statement of the objectives. Literally we say that to accomplish these objectives we will use these integrated systems. Hence, what is a partial total systems may provide the needed results. Our problem may resolve into that of determining precisely and completely the total objectives of the enterprise. This sets the stage for the total systems concept. The day of total systems may not have arrived as yet, but it surely is on its way. As experience, greater skill, and better techniques are developed for systems, along with continued progress in processing equipment, the present hurdles to far-reaching and inclusive integrated systems will be surmounted.

TOTAL MANAGEMENT INFORMATION SYSTEM

The ultimate of the total systems concept has been referred to by some as the Total Management Information System. This would include the entire enterprise and by means of systematic collecting, processing, and distributing of data would provide all necessary information to each individual in order to give maximum assistance in attaining specific goals. This is to say that each individual is given the information he needs to discharge effectively his responsibilities, to delegate to others his right to make decisions, and to facilitate all the fundamental functions of office management at all organizational levels.

Because interpretation of "what information is necessary" poses one of the biggest obstacles to a Total Management Information System, let us discuss further this requirement. To identify what information is necessary requires a rigidly monitored approach which stimulates employees to give serious thought to the problem. Simply asking for a statement of their informational needs usually results in incomplete answers, raises questions in the respondents' minds about costs, systems capabilities, means of processing, priorities, and attitudes of superiors. A satisfactory approach is to request each individual to provide answers to the following questions and in this sequence:

1. Specifically, what are your main work objectives?
2. For these work objectives, what are your principal responsibilities?
3. In keeping with these responsibilities, what types of decisions are you called upon to make?
4. What information do you feel you need to reach these decisions from the short-range viewpoint? From the long-range viewpoint? From within the enterprise? From outside the enterprise? From an idealistic viewpoint? From a practical viewpoint?
5. What are the key factors that throttle the work that you are supposed to do?
6. Classify the identified information given in answer to question No. 4 above into the following groups:
   a) Absolutely essential.
   b) Essential.
   c) Desirable.
   d) Helpful but really not needed.

Restrictions as to length of answers are in order as this promotes clarity and conciseness and facilitates review. Answers to question No. 4 are vital. The sequence provided builds up to this key question. Answers to questions No. 5 and No. 6 are related. Knowing the key factors (question No. 5) helps to classify the information (question No. 6).

Excellent examples of what can be considered total management information systems are found in the U.S. Air Force. They are the Management Control System (MCS) and the Strategic Air Command (SAC). These are total systems encompassing total operations although they are operated by a subagency. If not truly all-encompassing in their scope, they come very close to it. They are inclusive in keeping with their stated objectives. Also worthy of mention is the total logistics system of the U.S. Air Force. It is worldwide, totally integrated, and covers supply and maintenance. By its operation, service has been upgraded, yet enormous dollar savings have been realized.

The other military services have also been active in developing total management information systems. Both the U.S. Army and the U.S. Navy have active offices of management information. The Department of the Navy's office of management information consists of three top directorships, or organization units, as shown in Figure 17. The activities of each unit are clearly indicated in the figure. The reporting of naval program planning and execution by the operating agencies is in essence the makeup of the management information. The office of management

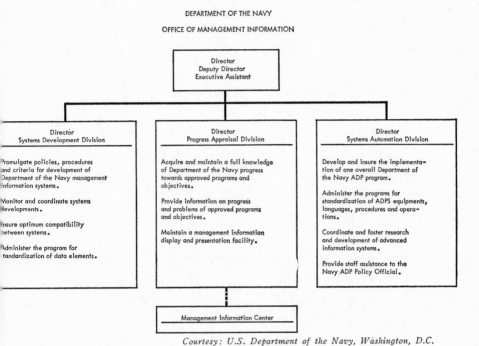

DEPARTMENT OF THE NAVY

OFFICE OF MANAGEMENT INFORMATION

Director
Deputy Director
Executive Assistant

Director
Systems Development Division

Promulgate policies, procedures and criteria for development of Department of the Navy management information systems.

Monitor and coordinate systems developments.

Insure optimum compatibility between systems.

Administer the program for standardization of data elements.

Director
Progress Appraisal Division

Acquire and maintain a full knowledge of Department of the Navy progress towards approved programs and objectives.

Provide information on progress and problems of approved programs and objectives.

Maintain a management information display and presentation facility.

Director
Systems Automation Division

Develop and insure the implementation of one overall Department of the Navy ADP program.

Administer the programs for standardization of ADPS equipments, languages, procedures and operations.

Coordinate and foster research and development of advanced information systems.

Provide staff assistance to the Navy ADP Policy Official.

Management Information Center

Courtesy: U.S. Department of the Navy, Washington, D.C.

FIG. 17. Makeup of the Office of Management Information of the U.S. Navy.

information develops systems to generate pertinent information and to help identify problems for top executives of the department.

Available in current literature is an example of what a machinery manufacturer, Farrel Corporation, is doing about a total management information system for improving its profit possibilities and controls.[2] The informational needs of planning, engineering, manufacturing, selling, and financing are integrated and designed to (1) give adequate and consistent planning and engineering documentation for each product line,

[2] "What Farrel Corporation Is Doing To Maintain and Improve Its Competitive Position," pamphlet published following annual stockholders meeting (Rochester, N.Y.: The Farrel Corporation, March 19, 1964).

(2) provide needed manufacturing information including purchasing data, schedules, and labor costs, (3) expedite sales forecasting, market penetration, and sales analyses, and (4) facilitate all fundamental finance information including accounts receivable, accounts payable, expenses, payroll checks, and standard cost data and control. With this unified arrangement, the managers of Farrel Corporation believe advantages well worthwhile will be realized including a reduction of materials cost, better manpower utilization, improved flexibility in scheduling, shorter manufacturing cycles, shorter sales delivery periods, improved customer services, and better collection of accounts receivable. With all these gains, the ability to handle a greater volume of business with existent facilities seems likely. Also the new system should supply a broader and deeper knowledge of the enterprise and its behavior as a unit. Figure 18 is a graphic representation of the system.

TOTAL SYSTEMS IMPACT UPON MANAGER'S RESPONSIBILITIES

From what has been stated it can be concluded that the use of total systems has an important impact upon a manager's responsibilities. By its adoption the area of decision making formerly given over to middle managers is greatly reduced. For example, decisions dealing with man-hour requirements, work scheduling, the timing and amount of reordering, and machine loading are highly circumscribed. In some instances they are removed from human beings and performed automatically by machines as prescribed by the system. The result is not an adjustment, but an elimination of the middle manager, for these areas are no longer subjected to his judgment and choice.

The need for thorough and adequate planning is emphasized by total systems. In this approach, we are dealing with too large an area to follow a "muddling through" practice. We must know where we are going and how we are going to get there. Not only is breadth of area alone important, but also the changing of relationships among the components, the elimination of some components, and the addition of others to the total picture are equally crucial. The disruptive influences can be large. The risk is high. Hence, to keep the risk and bad influences within known and reasonable limits, planning is resorted to and the determination of future activities is set forth.

Total systems usage tends to promote effective personnel relations. Responsibilities are better identified and known; cooperation is enhanced. The sense of being a part of a worthwhile total effort, of being expected to perform a specific and essential part of the entire work, and of doing it satisfactorily, help to provide an enthusiastic work group and a harmony of interest among the personnel.

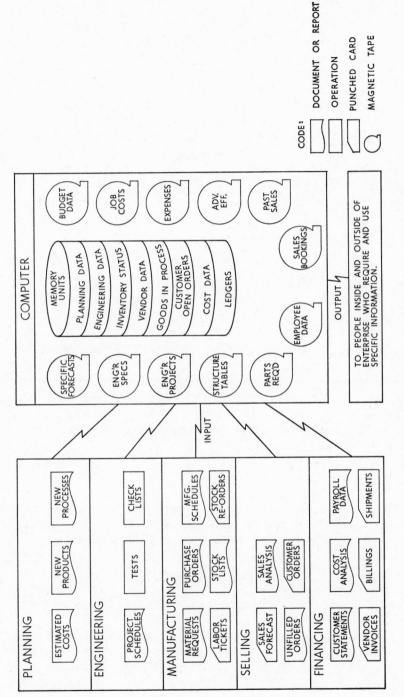

FIG. 18. One concept of a total management information system.

CHAPTER FOUR

THE PROCESSING OF

OFFICE WORK

To be a giant, and not a dwarf in your profession,
you must always be growing. The man that has ceased to
go up intellectually has begun to go down.
—William Mathews

HAVING accomplished via systems and procedures the total and mental image of what office work is to be done by automated means, let us now turn our attention to the actual processing of the work. It is this phase of office work with which most of us are somewhat familiar. We spend far more time and energy working with papers than we realize. Studies reveal, for example, that spending 15 percent of our work time with papers is common and in the case of some executives the figure skyrockets to 75 percent and more.

OBJECTIVES

Our objectives, or what we are trying to accomplish, are vital in determining what work process to follow. Likewise, objectives are vital in the designing of systems, procedures, and methods, and this was implied in the discussion of the last several chapters. However, objectives become more tangible when dealing with the selection and the evaluation of actual processes followed, and especially so when the work cycle is already in operation, but what we are getting from it appears inadequate or short of maximum effectiveness.

An interesting illustration concerns the U.S. Navy. Reports, forms, files, manuals, and procedures threatened to develop into a gigantic paper peak that could seriously damage naval combat readiness. Accordingly a project called SCRAP (Selective Curtailment of Reports and Paperwork) was started by the Navy in 1964. Its objective: "The prompt and drastic reduction of paperwork in the operating forces to that required by a Need to Know or Need to Act." Initial efforts were directed to three areas: (1) reports and forms, (2) directives, catalogs, and external correspondence, and (3) internal correspondence. To date excellent results have been achieved. Illustrative of "selective curtailment" accomplished is that 30 of

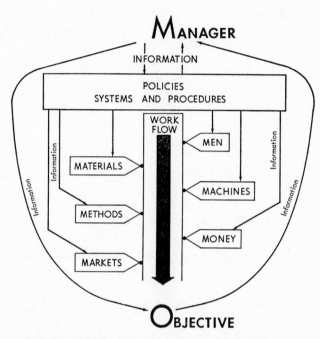

FIG. 19. Utilizing information, the manager formulates policies, systems, and procedures which guide the actions of the basic resources—men, materials, machines, methods, money, and markets—toward the objective. In turn, information is reported back to the manager of the accomplishment of the work flow so that adjustments, if necessary, can be made.

61 field activities have been relieved of preparing lengthy, complicated, and costly monthly reports.

Figure 19 shows the means by which a manager's efforts are directed toward accomplishing the objective. By means of information a manager establishes the policies, systems, and procedures to be utilized, which in turn guide the utilization of the basic resources of men, materials, machines, methods, money, and markets. The consolidated force of these resources moves and directs the work flow toward the objective. The effectiveness of this work flow is revealed by information returned to the manager, who can, if necessary, adjust the policies, systems, or procedures. The cycle is continuous: information for policies, systems, and procedures; for basic resources; for work flow evaluation; for policies, systems, and procedures.

TYPES OF OBJECTIVES

Indefinite, overly generalized, and difficult-to-measure objectives accomplish very little. "To improve paper work efforts," while commendable, is of little value in establishing guidelines and channeling efforts. We need specifics, such as which paper work, in which departments, and what reasonable expectancies. We can use the term *result* objective to identify those objectives that set forth the end accomplishment. That is, they emphasize what we want to achieve. Frequently they are expressed in general terms. In contrast, there are *how-to* objectives which stress the means for realizing the end goals. How-to objectives are more complex, more specific, and more difficult to state, but exceedingly helpful and, in fact, necessary for accomplishment of result objectives.

Objectives may be specific or general, written or unwritten, long or short term, temporary or permanent, or applicable to certain segments of the office only. Whatever their form or content, these objectives are set and accepted, for without them the meaning of management becomes nebulous and there is no satisfactory basis for determining the effectiveness of management.

Office objectives can also be classified as pertaining primarily to (1) service, (2) social responsibilities, or (3) profit. Service is of foremost importance in the objectives of managing office work because this work is done to assist others in doing their work more effectively. Also of significance is the objective dealing with social responsibilities which stresses the attainment of the goal in accordance with certain moral and ethical codes as set forth by the industry and society in which the enterprise operates. Lastly objectives emphasizing profit or gain to the owners can be assisted tremendously by office management. Performing the office work more effectively can mean more profit inasmuch as lower expenditures for clerical work are made. Greater emphasis of the importance of the office to management and profit is in order. Acceptance of this obligation by office management members strengthens their status and identifies their role.[1]

---

[1] The concept of profit as the objective of any enterprise or segment of an enterprise is actually quite limited. Profit, as such, can be the indirect or the direct aim, depending upon the thinking of the particular company involved. Profit is residual in nature, a by-product resulting from other direct goals.

INFORMATION AND OFFICE WORK

The question can be asked, "Why process data?" The answer: To provide information. This simple answer is fundamental and it represents the ultimate and real essence of office automation. Information is the most comprehensive and meaningful result of office work as it is popularly used. The processing is performed to provide proper and adequate information to the right person at the right time and in the right form. Wherever office work is done, there is a fountainhead of information. This is what makes data processing so important. This is why office work is growing so rapidly. This is the reason so much effort is being expended on how office work should be performed.

WHAT IS INFORMATION?

Information is meaningful data—words, figures, or symbols—that convey usable knowledge. What is usable depends upon the following:

1. *Objective of the recipient.* If information is to help, it must assist the recipient in what he is trying to do.

2. *Accuracy of the data transmission and processing.* The real essence and significance of the information must be retained regardless of how it is handled and manipulated.

3. *Time.* Is the information current? Does it have maximum value by virtue of being the latest available?

4. *Space or place.* Is the information available at the right place? This implies that the information is supplied to the proper recipients.

5. *Form.* Can the information be used effectively? Does it show needed relationships, trends, and areas requiring managerial attention; and does it emphasize pertinent situations?

6. *Semantics.* Is the relationship between the words and their intended meaning absolutely clear? Is there any likelihood of misunderstanding? The word "duck," for example, may mean a type of cloth, a type of fowl, or to move quickly.

It is well to point out that, as defined above, not all data are information. There are today many useless records and reports being prepared and distributed. In contrast, there are gaps of information that need to be bridged by useful data. Generally, it is the responsibility of the office manager, administrative manager, or whatever his title, to supply needed information in order that the entire enterprise can be managed efficiently.

INFORMATION DEVELOPMENT

Information is supplied either to a manager or a nonmanager. What information is supplied depends upon the recipient's job, but in any event it should be what the recipient needs, wants, and uses, qualified by what information is available and feasible to obtain. The recipient, together with the information compiler, should decide what information to provide. In these efforts, however, the quantity of information must be carefully controlled. This is an especially important consideration today when, by means of computers and other electronic machines, it is possible to compile information in 15 minutes that takes a man two days to read and two weeks to assimilate.

In addition, there are new requirements placing greater and greater demands upon the supplying of information. A number of factors are responsible. High on the list is the growth and complexity of enterprises. As companies expand, merge, and diversify, there is a greater need for formal information to keep personnel adequately informed. Another contributing cause is the growth in the number of executives. The trend is toward more management members over specialized areas, and this necessitates the distribution of information to a wide range of executives within relatively short periods. Also, the force of competition, both domestic and foreign, can be cited. The managers of a company, for example, may have to decide where to locate a branch factory or warehouse for maximum marketing impact. The information requirements necessary to reach this decision are large and involve digestion of a considerable number of facts. In addition, the increasing expenditures for research and development, and the resulting new processes and new products, accelerate the need for accurate information on financial needs, production activities, and other phases of a business. In turn, these changes increase the complexity of the information and emphasize the need to schedule efforts economically. Lastly, information of various types has been developed because it is required of enterprises by government. In this catgory are data relating to taxes, and compliance with regulations and numerous legal requirements. Without proper information, managers are unable to comply with the law.

In brief, information development has come about because today's mode of operation simply does not permit either the successful manager or the successful nonmanager to carry in his head all the information needed to carry out his work effectively. The manager needs information on cost, sales, production, personnel, plans, accomplishments, inventories, machines, customers, prices, markets, and taxes. The nonmanager requires work instructions, scheduling data, deadline dates, evaluation of efforts, and notices of work changes. These represent masses of data which must be collected and put into easily accessible form in order to have maximum value and benefit. Also, it should be pointed out that machine availability to handle the information quickly and properly is contributing toward the status of information development. For several decades there has been a continuous parade of new office machines designed to accomplish office work more efficiently. And the pace is quickening. Computers are making deep modifications in office work methodology, and they are destined to cause even greater changes in the future.

SUPPLYING INFORMATION

Supplying needed information requires fundamentally four activities. These include data (1) collecting, (2) processing, (3) retaining, and (4) distributing. Figure 20 shows this concept graphically. First of all, the

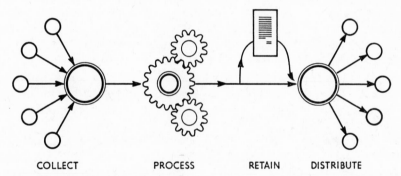

COLLECT   PROCESS   RETAIN   DISTRIBUTE

FIG. 20.   Data must be collected, processed, retained, and distributed to provide information needed to manage an enterprise effectively.

data must be collected; and, as discussed in the following paragraphs, there exist major sources of data in most enterprises. Next, the collected data must be processed. In brief, the descriptive information must be arranged according to a predetermined pattern, numerical values must be calculated, and helpful relationships must be shown. Typically, some information is either retained by the office for additional data, when available, to be added to what has been processed, or is retained simply for future reference purposes. Lastly, the processed data are distributed to those requiring the information and include all types of communication. More will now be discussed for each of these four activities.

THE COLLECTING OF DATA

Practically every operation in a modern enterprise gives rise to data. While the terms may differ from enterprise to enterprise, depending upon the type of enterprise, the following operations or activities can be considered basic sources of data.

Operation or Activity	Gives Rise to Need for:
Purchasing	Vendors' list, prices, quotations, delivery dates
Receiving	Receipt of material, inspection, quantity
Stockkeeping	On hand, coming in, location, allocation
Production	Process times, orders, waiting times
Selling	Customers' orders, sales analysis, price
Delivery	Date, carrier information, bills of lading
Billing	Customer's name, merchandise, price
Collecting	Credit, invoice, discounts
Disbursing	Payroll, materials purchased, taxes

Actually, all this type of information is obtained from data expressed as words, numbers, and symbols. The challenge is to put the proper data together and make them available to the proper party at the proper time. For instance, under purchasing, for a vendors' list to be useful, it should contain (1) names, preferably alphabetically, by type of commodity or by location; (2) terms of sale; (3) past experience with vendor; (4) name of representative with vendor; and (5) telephone number. Likewise, certain data must be put together meaningfully for (say) billing, collecting, and disbursing.

THE PROCESSING OF DATA

Data processing is a series of planned operations upon information in order to achieve a desired objective or result. Usually, a step-by-step arrangement, a formula, or pattern is followed to arrive at a result that shows the data in some standard and useful form. Bookkeeping, inventory record keeping, payroll, accounting, and the solving of mathematical equations are all included under the heading of processing of data.

The performance of the operations in predetermined sequence and the devices or machines employed to perform these operations constitute a data-processing system. There are many types of devices and hence many types of data-processing systems, that can be employed. For example:

1. The device may be simply pen and paper.
2. The device may be an adding machine and an accounting machine.
3. The device may be a computer.

Likewise, the sequence of operations may differ from one system to another, depending largely upon the goal and the devices to be utilized. However, regardless of the data-processing system, *the plan of processing is always of human origin.* Furthermore, the system is, or should be, performed essentially to serve human beings. Data are processed to put them into a form that has greatest utilization.

BASIC ELEMENTS OF DATA PROCESSING

Specifically, what are some basic elements of data processing? In answering this question, many will mention "writing" and "calculating," and a few will include "storing." But study of the processing effort reveals that there are not three but eight basic elements of processing. These are shown in Figure 21. The reason each element is performed and the result obtained from applying each element to the data are also included in the figure. To illustrate, sorting (No. 4) is performed to classify the data and results in the data being related to one or more bases.

It would be difficult to overstate the importance of these basic elements of data processing. They serve as the nucleus around which all paper work revolves. Various combinations of these elements, in kind as well as in degree, are required to supply the needed information which the office is expected to furnish.

PROCESSING AND PRODUCTION UNIT EMPLOYED

The development and use of the modern electronic computer has brought emphasis and recognition to the basic elements of data processing. Terminology such as "input," "output," "transmitting," and "recording" is commonplace with computer installations. However, these terms are actually not exclusive with computer usage. These elements of processing are basic and universal. They exist in all data processing, whether noncomputer processing or computer processing.

To highlight this important fact, Figure 22 is included. In this figure, the basic elements of data processing are shown across the top, while the common office productive units are listed vertically in the left column.[2] The basic elements of processing performed by each production unit are indicated by the check marks. For example, an accounting machine performs the basic elements of writing, recording, sorting, calculating, and comparing. In contrast, a copying machine performs just one basic element of processing—recording. A human being performs all the basic elements of data processing.

---

[2] Office production units or machines are discussed in detail in Chapters 5 and 7.

Basic Element of Data Processing	Why Performed	Results in:
1. Reading	To interpret data by going over characters, words, and symbols	Awareness of data existence
2. Writing, typing, card punching, or paper-tape perforating (frequently called *input*)	To facilitate processing by putting data on or in medium, i.e., alphabetical or numerical marks on paper, holes in paper, magnetic areas on tape, and magnetic ink on paper	Start of data processing
3. Recording or printing (frequently called *output*)	To obtain results of processing, the data—in medium form for processing purposes—are converted to form easily read by a human being, if not already in that form	End of data processing
4. Sorting	To classify the data	Data being related to one or more bases
5. Transmitting	To disseminate the data	Data availability for specific purpose and place
6. Calculating	To manipulate the data mathematically	Numerical data being added, subtracted, multiplied, or divided
7. Comparing	To check data for accuracy and completeness	Quantitative and qualitative inspection of data
8. Storing	To retain or keep the data	Data being available when needed

Note: The meaning of each of the following terms, frequently used in office management, is included in the above listing:

a) "Interpreting" (usually associated with No. 2 or No. 3) is imprinting the meaning of the punched holes in a punched card on that card.

b) "Reproducing" (usually associated with No. 2) is duplicating an exact copy of a punched card.

c) "Collating" (usually associated with No. 4) is merging sets of related data into a single set.

d) "Segregating" (usually associated with No. 4) is separating sets of related data into several sets.

FIG. 21.   The basic elements of data processing.

This figure helps to identify the makeup of information. It assists in grasping the important overall picture of what is managed in the office and in understanding better the role and operation of various office production units. It also demonstrates that what has been done with papers for years is still being done, whether essentially by hand, by ordinary office machine, or by computer.

THE RETAINING OF DATA

The very nature and reason-to-be of much paper work requires that data be retained. The more obvious reason is to keep it for future

BASIC ELEMENT OF DATA PROCESSING

OFFICE PRODUCTION UNIT EMPLOYED	READING 1	WRITING, TYPING, ETC. 2	RECORDING, PRINTING 3	SORTING 4	TRANSMITTING 5	CALCULATING 6	COMPARING 7	STORING 8
ACCOUNTING MACHINE		V	V	V		V	V	
ADDING AND CALCULATING MACHINES		V	V			V		
ADDRESSING MACHINE			V	V				
COMPUTER WITHOUT SPECIAL ATTACHMENT			V	V	V	V	V	V
COPYING MACHINE			V					
ELECTRONIC READER	V	V						
HUMAN BEING	V	V	V	V	V	V	V	V
MICROFILM UNITS			V					V
PNEUMATIC TUBE					V			
PUNCHING MACHINE		V						
SORTER				V				
TABULATOR			V		V	V	V	
TELAUTOGRAPH		V	V		V			
TELEGRAPH		V	V		V			
TELETYPEWRITER		V	V		V			
TYPEWRITER		V	V					

FIG. 22. Each office production unit performs specific basic elements of data processing.

reference. The decision regarding what to retain, for how long a period, and under what arrangement is a vital part of providing needed information. However, equally important is the retaining of data either mentally, manually, or mechanically so that subsequent data can be appended to the already existing fund and thus keep the information current.

The retaining of data for subsequent processing and bringing them up to date has been emphasized by the use of the computer—the function of its so-called memory unit. But data retention is also basic in paper work performed by hand, in placing papers in a file so that they can be located easily for future reference, or where records are kept solely in the owner's head.

THE DISTRIBUTING OF DATA

Collecting, processing, and, when necessary, retaining data are insufficient for information to be utilized by employees and customers. The information must also be distributed to those who have need for it. This task includes the proper placing and timing of the information. It includes all the means of communication such as mail, telephone, telegraph, inter-communication systems, and electronic communication devices.

An employee's effectiveness depends upon the accuracy, timeliness, and precision with which his contribution is geared to the overall plan. When this thesis is followed, reports are distributed only to employees who are in a position to take direct action; only information which, directly or indirectly, helps get the job done is provided. Violations of these rules in the distributing of data are common sources of inefficiency in information handling.

CHARACTERISTICS OF OFFICE WORK

Pointing out the important distinguishing features about work performed for informational purposes serves to supply the concept of what is being managed in the area of office management. Accordingly, the major characteristics of this work will now be discussed.

1. *A facilitating function.* Office work is a facilitating function; it is the essential medium through which the various activities of an enterprise are fused together. In a sense, office work can be called the "catalytic agent" of modern management.[3]

The work of the office assists in efforts to increase output, lower costs, stimulate employees, pay wages, purchase materials, and ship orders. The individual work of practically every department in an enterprise is implemented by office work. For example, a credit department cannot operate successfully without current records of creditors, amounts and dates due, lists of delinquent accounts, credit histories of customers, and a quantity of correspondence.

Of special importance is the facilitating action of office work in decision making. Information is gathered and analyzed in relation to a set of alternative solutions to a problem in order to reach a decision. Likewise, information is the basis for communicating. For example, the exchanging of ideas and suggestions among people to develop the alternatives, the reporting of the decision to others so that implementation can take place, and the reporting back to evaluate what is being accomplished are all predicated upon communicating.

---

[3] "Catalytic agent" is a term used in chemistry and means an element the presence of which is necessary to bring about a desired reaction between other elements but which does not itself enter into the reaction. In a similar manner, office work brings about a desired reaction of business elements but does not enter into the reaction itself.

2. *A service work.* Another distinguishing feature of office work is that it is a service work. In and of itself, office work serves little purpose; it is performed to help others do their work more effectively. For example, office work is a service to the top executive officers, to the production department, to the sales department, and to the finance department. It helps supply top executives with data which are necessary in order to manage the enterprise. By means of records, the production department is helped to improve its service and to lower costs, the sales department is aided in its work of selling the product, and the finance department is assisted in maintaining written evidence of the financial status of the enterprise.

Unfortunately this concept is frequently overlooked. In their zeal to improve office efforts, some embrace the thought that information is the end product and that giving it to the proper personnel insures that the desired action will result therefrom immediately. This is tremendously misleading. Most managers and nonmanagers are not concerned primarily with securing, processing, and giving information. They have other important work to do. The information they receive is supposed to help them do their respective jobs. The intent is to keep them effective in their particular area and in doing what they are hired to do, namely, managing, selling, performing production work, or financing, and not in preparing, reading, or discussing reports and records.

Service is the primary objective of the office. Consideration for office costs, as well as for the utility, quality, and quantity of the office services, is also important; but these should be recognized as secondary objectives. An eagerness to slash all costs or a decision to compile only records which the office believes are useful might result in failure to provide the necessary office services to the other departments. Thus, losses occur in these departments that probably far exceed the savings in operation. However, the service should be evaluated in terms of cost; elaborate and excessive service usually means waste, while, on the other hand, inadequate service represents false economy.

3. *Volume determined by outside.* Unlike many major business activities, the volume of office work is determined by factors outside the office. These factors include the number of shipments, the amount of collections, the number of open accounts, the quantity of sales letters, the number of factory employees, and the number of items manufactured or sold—all factors outside the control of the office.

This unique characteristic makes for problems in information handling. For example, provisions for fluctuations in the work load must be provided, even though the timing and extent of the variation are wide and usually cannot be accurately forecast. Also more often than not decisions made by nonoffice management members and about which the office management member has little or nothing to say affect significantly the work managed by the office management members.

4. *An indirect contributor to profit.* No profit is realized directly from office work, since it acts through the operative departments, such as the production, sales, and finance departments.[4] In this sense, office work contributes indirectly, not directly, to the profit-making ability of the enterprise. However, some feel that office work produces profit. This belief stems primarily from considering the office as a complete unit within itself.

However, the fact that the office does not contribute directly to profit making means that it is usually on the defensive insofar as justifying expenditures is concerned. It is, for example, unlike sales, where by spending so much it is hoped to realize a resultant gain in sales and also in profits. In dealing with the management of office work we must constantly seek to justify the work and its cost and to point out wherein it is good management to make the expenditure.

5. *Contents.* The predominant type of work making up office work is typing and calculating. Various studies reveal that these two types account for nearly one-half of all office time. Other important activities include checking or proofing, filing, telephoning, programming, duplicating, and mailing and these, together with typing and calculating, constitute nearly 90 percent of office employees' work time. As office mechanization advances this pattern changes somewhat, but it is interesting to note that typing remains a very essential activity whether manual, semimechanized, or full automation of performing office work is followed. This is due to the fact that currently typing is usually necessary to put the input information into a form acceptable for receiving by the machine. However, as we employ more machines that read and convert ordinary written data into "machine language," the volume of typing probably will decline.

6. *Dispersion.* Office work is not performed exclusively in any one department; some of it is performed in every department of an enterprise. The swing to mechanization, and especially to computers, has resulted in much office work being handled within a single location; but there is still considerable paper work in other areas—for example, in the purchasing, engineering, or inspection department. Furthermore, a milling machine operator in a factory usually performs some clerical work in the normal course of his daily duty. Where financial incentives and production control are used, the operator may be responsible for a considerable amount of

---

[4] "Profit," as used here, is the residual income accruing to the owner of an enterprise after he has paid all the economic aids of production—that is, rent on all land used, interest on all capital used, and wages to all labor used.

clerical work, yet he is not classified as an office worker. Likewise, most salesmen are accountable for sizable amounts of paper work; and the same is true of many employees of a personnel department, who are quick to point out the voluminous paper work used in the execution of their tasks.

Figure 23 indicates the dispersion of paper work and the basic

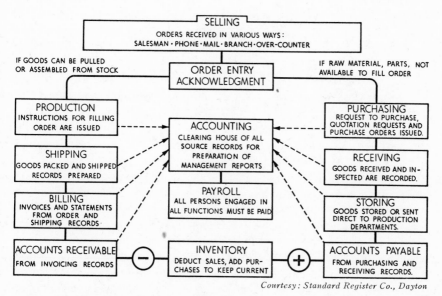

Courtesy: Standard Register Co., Dayton

FIG. 23. Records permeate an entire enterprise. Information is required by every department.

functions of business. Selling gives rise to the order entry acknowledgment, and the subsequent paper work flow affects many departments, whether the goods are shipped or assembled from stock, or needed raw materials are obtained to take care of the customer's order. What we are saying is that information is required by people throughout an entire organization, as well as by certain others outside the organization, in order for the enterprise to function effectively.

7. *Personnel performing.* One of the interesting developments among office employees is the increasing proportion of women in this category. In the year 1870, for example, only 2 percent of office personnel were women; by 1930, the percentage was nearly 50; by 1950, the number of women office employees reached 60 percent of the total; and in 1965, women held nearly 71 percent of all office jobs.

There is, however, a tendency for certain office jobs to be occupied by men. These include accountant, programmer, analyst, collection clerk, credit clerk, and correspondent. Other office jobs are commonly held by women. In this group are the jobs of file clerk, machine operator, tape librarian, receptionist, typist, stenographer, and telephone operator. Still other jobs are held by either men or women and include those of bookkeeper, cashier, mail clerk, and private secretary.

Also, the proportion of office workers to total workers varies considerably with different industries. For example, nearly one-half of the workers in finance, insurance, and real estate are office workers. In contrast, the proportion is about 11 percent in manufacturing and only 0.3 percent in agriculture, forestry, and fisheries.

GROWTH OF INFORMATION HANDLING

An interesting fact in connection with office work processing and its automation is that information development has taken place quite rapidly. The growth has been especially sharp during the past several decades. The number of people engaged in paper work increased approximately 138 percent from 1940 to 1965, while during this same period, total population increased 48 percent and the total working force expanded 56 percent.

Why this tremendous growth? One major consideration is the industrial growth of the United States with its specialization and its need for other activities to keep the industrial growth virile. For example, during the period 1900–1960, the number engaged in manufacturing occupations increased from 6 million to 16.4 million, and the number engaged in "service industries" spurted from 4 million to nearly 14 million. We commonly associate the growth of our economy with manufacturing efficiency—improved methods, better machines, and more effective controls. But this growth has brought with it expenditures sometimes overlooked in that obtaining, processing, and distributing information for attaining these manufacturing gains costs nearly as much as does the direct production labor.

Likewise, growth in government has been mentioned as a cause for the increase in information handling. To supply the ever expanding requests by government for information necessitates more and more office work within private enterprises. Also, from the government's side, both the amount of its clerical work and the number of governmental office employees have also increased. Estimates are that there were nearly 5 million office workers in public administration work in 1965.

Finally, some portion of the growth in office personnel and office work is undoubtedly due to inadequate efforts to control it. The preparation of essential paper work only, the extended use of efficient office machines, the adequate motivation of office employees, and the development of proper systems, procedures, and methods are examples of efforts which assist in reducing the amount of paper work.

WILL GROWTH CONTINUE?

Opinions differ regarding the future growth of information handling. Some believe it will continue to grow at a rate exceeding that of all other types of work. They view it as basically a self-perpetuating situation—more people, more paper; more paper, more people. They point out that we have become attuned to the use of the products of the office.

In contrast, many believe that the upward trend in office work cannot continue. They insist we are drowning in a sea of paper and that some office work has become a ritual performance for its own sake. They observe that the past increase in office work has resulted in an overwhelming increase in overhead costs and that this process cannot continue indefinitely.

THE FUTURE OF THE OFFICE

A number of available studies point out that there exists considerable waste office work. The exact amount is unknown, but the gains to be won by eliminating just a portion of this unnecessary processed information staggers the imagination. It seems that a simple approach could be followed: (1) Eliminate the unnecessary paper work being done, and (2) perform the necessary paper work more efficiently. The first criterion is to determine what office work serves effectively a definite and essential need, that is, provides essential information. Opinions, of course, will differ in this evaluation. The second criterion stresses such things as simplification of the office processes, training of office employees, and more office mechanization.

But an interesting paradox should be noted. Based on much of our experience to date, our ability to handle a large volume of paper work at a low unit cost, as exemplified by many mechanized processes, is actually a problem, not a solution. Enormous quantities of data are processed and made up into reports of all kinds, copies of papers are run off with little effort, and memoranda are quickly prepared. In each case copies are distributed to many members of the enterprise. Receipt of them signals the reading of them. This takes time as does subsequent thinking about them and answering or expressing opinions about them to others. In addition, the papers are filed, eventually the need for additional filing equipment is generated, and more floor space is needed. The net result is that what was thought and intended to decrease paper work actually has increased it. The answer lies in more rigid control of "what is necessary paper work" and this is essentially a human, not a machine contribution.

Increased emphasis will probably be placed upon analysis and interpretation of information made available by the office. As more facts are needed and can be made available within a reasonable period, the task of determining what data are necessary, and why, will take on new and increasing meaning. But the facilitating and service elements of office work will remain of prime importance. Determining and providing essential information effectively, and thus contributing to the success of the entire enterprise, will continue to be the vital task of office management.

Some feel that the whole concept of information needs drastic revision. In their opinion much of the present information is incomplete, too late, unreliable, and poorly organized to have maximum value. Facts for today's decisions reach managers next week. Reams of detailed data are supplied, but helpful summaries and relationships are lacking. Distinction between the critical and the immaterial is not indicated. The need is for a complete reorientation of information. What we now have is outmoded. In an economy such as ours, where manufacturing techniques, products, and markets change as rapidly as they do, we cannot operate an enterprise on fragmented and historical facts that are basically an extension of the past.

Certainly there are elements of truth in these contentions. The challenge is great and it is reasonable to assert that with the need and importance of information being increasingly recognized, fundamental changes for the better will evolve. Then too, there are some who believe the office of the future will not employ papers. Information will be supplied to a great extent by means of drums, tapes, and wires—media of certain office machines. To illustrate, payroll checks might be replaced with information fed by wire from the employer's machine directly into the bank's machine for credit to the individual employee's account. Collectors will receive payment by drawing on their customers' checking accounts. Whether these things come about is conjectural, but the trend toward greater mechanization is taking place.

As office mechanization increases, it would seem that clerical personnel will become more technically proficient, require more training, become more productive, and receive higher wages. But the many problems stemming from the relationship of the employee to a machine, the degree cialization, and the acquisition of work satisfaction by the e likely to be multiplied.

CHAPTER FIVE

WHAT EQUIPMENT AND
MACHINES TO USE

*He that will not reason is a bigot; he that cannot
reason is a fool; he that dares not reason is a slave.*
—*William Drummond*

THE KNOWLEDGE, selection, and use of proper equipment and machines are basic in office automation. The work must be accomplished in the proposed manner, sequence, and form which are in keeping with the plans derived by those in charge of information processing. Analysis and study of the various types of office equipment and machines are usually in order. The computer is, of course, the zenith of office machines. However, knowledge and understanding of all the essential equipment and machines available prove very helpful in determining what means to use for a given set of circumstances. As mentioned in Chapter 1, office automation can be thought of as the extension of mechanization and futhermore, so-called standard office machines can be integrated into a unit representing a high degree of office automation. The use of various office equipment and machines is popular and represents powerful forces in accomplishing office work.

SELECTION OF OFFICE EQUIPMENT AND MACHINES

The expanding use of office equipment and machines places an increasing burden and responsibility upon those in charge of data processing. They must marshal all available facts about possible facilities and help decide the best units in keeping with the particular requirements set forth by their systems, procedures, and methods planning. To illustrate, they need to know the types of equipment available, the characteristics of each, the cost per unit of output, the initial outlay, and the maintenance cost.

77

More fundamental, however, is to decide whether the equipment or machine is really needed. Does the volume, type, and occurrence of the work merit a mechanized means? If so, which one or ones should be employed. It may be advantageous to farm out the work to a service bureau specializing in the work involved.

Usually, careful evaluation of several aspects are required to select wisely a particular unit of office equipment or machine. The decision should never be made hastily or impulsively.

The sales representatives of most office equipment manufacturers are excellent sources of helpful information about their particular products. They are very willing to be of service and will cheerfully give or try to find out the information requested. The office manager will do well to work with them, for they can keep him informed of latest developments and advise him of any special applications in other offices. This may prove an important source of ideas for improvements. Furthermore, these representatives can help in working out special applications and uses. The representative should be considered as one who is trying to help. His aggressiveness adds to his merit, as this characteristic is desirable in sales representatives.

On the other hand, the office manager, or whoever selects office equipment or machines, has definite obligations to fulfill. Good management dictates that these objectives cannot be ignored, passed over lightly, or left entirely to the sales representative.

EQUIPMENT AND MACHINE SELECTION FACTORS

The following 12 factors should be carefully considered:

1. *The work and the manner of accomplishing it.* The purpose of the work should be clearly defined and critically examined, to assure that it is absolutely essential. Knowledge of what is probably the best way of doing the work, along with alternative effective ways, should be determined. Sometimes, work of a similar nature currently performed in the office can be used as a guide. The work and its manner of performance may strongly suggest a table rather than a desk be supplied, or a particular model of a machine be selected for it best answers the specific work requirements.

2. *The individual requirements.* The decision to utilize a particular piece of office equipment or machine should be based upon the *individual* requirements of the particular office. Use by others is not sufficient grounds for adoption. This is especially important in regard to office machines. The efficient office manager does not mechanize an office

operation whenever it is possible to do so. Instead, he considers the available machines in the light of the way each one will assist in getting the work accomplished in his particular office. Basing his decision upon these factual data, he decides what, if any, machine to utilize.

However, as implied in the chapters on office automation, there is emerging a universality of data processing and distributing adaptable for all enterprises. Consideration of these universal concepts of what is necessary and what is not, from the viewpoint of effective information handling via automation, may prove them quite adequate for the individual enterprise's requirements. It could well be that in certain cases, individual requirements are stressed too much, necessitating special and high-cost operations being added.

3. *Amount and value of total time saved.* A new office machine might foster greater speeds of accomplishment, but the important consideration is not comparison of speeds but savings in total time, both in amount and value. The amount will depend a great deal upon the volume of work. Economies are usually not realized unless the unit is operating a good portion of the time. In addition, the utilization of time saved must be evaluated. To be advantageous, time saved should be used for other productive office work. If the time saved is simply dissipated and spread over other tasks, there are no economic benefits.

4. *Flexibility of use.* The extent to which the units can be used for various types of work in the office governs the economies gained. Generally speaking, if a unit being considered can be used effectively for many types of office work, its adoption usually can be justified. Likewise, the feature of expansion and contraction in order to accommodate varying amounts of paper work is normally advantageous.

5. *Price and investment.* Price is always an important managerial consideration, but it should be considered along with the services made available by the unit. That is, consideration must be given to what is received as well as what is paid out. In many instances, purchases of equipment are made on the basis that expected savings will recoup the initial investment within about one-fourth the life of the unit.

However, the factors which determine how quickly an office unit should pay for itself vary somewhat with the policies of the individual purchaser and with the importance attached to each factor. Usually, the decision is based on an evaluation of such things as (*a*) the current complete price, including installation and delivery; (*b*) if a replacement, the make, model, type, and condition of the replaced unit and its probable current market value; (*c*) the percentage of working time the unit will be used; and (*d*) the investment percentage return to the company (the effect of income taxes and overhead expenses in reducing the gross earnings should be included in this calculation).[1]

Figure 24 shows a quick rule-of-thumb approach to decide whether to purchase a particular piece of office equipment or machine. It is based on timesaving by personnel, as illustrated by a ratio of personnel to equipment or machine. For example, the salary cost per minute for an employee receiving $5,000 a year is approximately 5 cents. The number of thousands of dollars per year is approximately the equivalent number of cents per minute. For a $10,000 accounting machine, the cost per working day is $4. Hence, $4 divided by 5 cents per minute gives 80 minutes as the

Salary per Year (1)	Approximate Salary per Minute (2)	Cost per Day for $10,000 Accounting Machine (3)	Personnel Time Required to Save (in Minutes) (4)
$ 5,000..............	5.0¢	$4.00	80.0
7,500..............	7.5	4.00	53.4
10,000..............	10.0	4.00	40.0
12,500..............	12.5	4.00	32.0
15,000..............	15.0	4.00	26.6

Column 2 is based on 250 working days a year, eight-hour day, and 83 percent efficiency.
Column 3 is based on 250 working days a year, ten-year life span.
Column 4 is Column 3 divided by Column 2.

FIG. 24.   A quick and convenient means of determining whether an office machine will pay for itself within a reasonable period. The approach is based on determining the time required to be saved by the employee who will use the machine.

time required to be saved by a $5,000 employee to pay for the accounting machine.

6. *Capacity of unit.* It is imperative that the unit be of sufficient size to permit efficient operations. Nothing is gained by getting a smaller desk or accounting machine than the reasonable expectancy of work volume indicates is necessary. In the case of many machines, the expected output can be judged from experience of actual users of the machine, data from the manufacturer, and actual test runs in the office. When feasible, this latter source is recommended; in fact, it is always advisable to obtain a demonstration of an office machine. Free trials, however, should be carefully qualified as to purpose, use, and extent of time; for unless this is done, a machine originally brought in for trial tends to remain, and eventual purchase may be required, regardless of selection efforts.

7. *Aesthetic values.* The appearance of the office—a desire to impress by having the latest or the finest in office equipment and machines—is an

---

[1] Depreciation and the influence of trade-ins are discussed later in this chapter.

important, although sometimes subdued or concealed, consideration. Aesthetic values are highly subjective; justification for certain selections is based on personal likes. Such values have a place, for office equipment and machines are not only a *physical* means of assisting employees to accomplish their work but also serve as a *mental* stimuli. Supplying the proper unit makes for a positive and cooperative attitude and helps place the employee in the right frame of mind to work efficiently.

8. *Employee preference.* This consideration is of great significance because the human element is vital in determining whether the equipment is properly utilized or operated. A strong bias against a particular unit prevents maximum benefits from being realized, regardless of the suitability of the unit to the work. The highly successful office manager will not force the use of a particular unit against a prejudice which the employee may have concerning that unit. Most office employees will turn out consistently the maximum work of acceptable quality when they are supplied with the equipment and machines *they feel* are the best available.

9. *Effect upon personnel requirements.* In many cases, the installation of office equipment or machines changes the requirements regarding both the number of employees and the level of their skill; and the problems of transferring, reducing, and training the work force must be considered. For example, in the case of machines, trained operators or the availability of those who are trainable as operators are foremost considerations. Furthermore, when machines are adopted to perform monotonous work, the effect upon personnel is also important, because usually a happier and more satisfied work force is the result.

10. *Forecast of work load.* As in all planning, not only must the current volume and type of work be considered, but also the probable future requirements and the adequacy of the unit to fulfill these future needs. Future requirements should be estimated for about five years, and such forecasts are sometimes quite difficult. Good management requires, however, that the unit neither become inadequate to handle the work volume several months after its installation nor stand idle a large portion of the time because of a decline in work volume which could have been predetermined.

11. *Quality of paper work.* The effect of the unit upon the accuracy and appearance of the papers should also be considered. When a machine is to replace a manual operation, increased accuracy usually will result, for machines tend to make fewer errors than human beings. Also, forms executed by machine generally have a better appearance; they are neater, more legible, and more uniform than papers which are handwritten.

12. *Need for copies and statistical data.* This consideration applies mainly to office machines selection. A contemplated machine may provide

more copies of a record, and it may furnish a great deal of data of a sort and in a form not currently available. However, the important consideration is whether these available copies and data are necessary and whether they serve useful purposes which significantly aid management efforts.

DEPRECIATION AND TRADE-IN

There is no one set of answers to the questions of how to figure depreciation and when it is economically sound to purchase a machine or to make a trade-in. The planner must refer to the accounting practices followed. Most companies consider office equipment and machines as assets; and over a period, they write them off because of depreciation. The period will depend upon the kind of product. For example, the following are common:

```
Desks............................20 years
Files..............................15   "
Accounting machines...................10   "
Rugs and carpets.....................10   "
Typewriters......................... 5   "
```

The rate used over the period can be calculated by various methods. Straight line and sum-of-digits are common, but the new "guideline form," permitted by present tax laws and designed to encourage new purchases, is gaining favor. Some companies follow the practice of charging to expense any equipment purchase of less than a stated amount, for example, $100; and any equipment purchase over this amount is put into an assets account. Other practices are also followed, but they must be reasonable and within the meaning and intent of income tax laws.

Some general overall guiding policy for trade-ins should be followed, tempered with certain adjustments based upon the individual circumstances. Several main factors influence a trade-in. First is the availability of the cash and capital resources of the enterprise. This is always present in any trade-in discussion. Second are the expected cash savings to be derived from the new unit's use. If these savings will pay for the net outlay within 24 months, a trade-in is usually in order. Third is the difference between the accrued net depreciation and the expense necessary to keep the unit operating. If the net (present book value minus trade-in) is less than the cost of repair, a trade-in is probably best.

BUY OR LEASE

At one time, only certain types of office equipment and machines could be obtained on a leasing basis. Now, the practice of leasing has spread to practically every type of office facility. Details of leasing agreements vary widely. For example, some grant a right to purchase, after leasing for a period of time, commonly three to five years, by crediting a portion of the lease payments toward the purchase price.

Advocates of the leasing basis claim better maintenance is provided and the leasee is free from the expense and worry of keeping all units in top operating condition. In addition, leasing permits capital to be utilized in other more productive facilities. A large portion of the leasee's funds are not tied up in long-term equipment and machine needs. Furthermore, leasing permits the payments to be considered as expenses from the tax viewpoint, not as assets, as is the case with purchase. To some companies, this can be a distinct advantage. Also, leasing supplies units to meet temporary or fill-in needs. Flexibility is provided. Then too, leasing makes feasible trial usage of units. It is helpful to find out how the unit will work out before purchasing it. In contrast, many managers always buy equipment and machines if it is possible to do so. They state that in the long run, purchasing is less costly than leasing, they are free to move the facility as they like, and they can arrive independently at decisions affecting equipment or machines. Also, it should be noted that if funds are available, investment in equipment and machines in one's own business can be attractive.

MAINTENANCE

All office equipment and machines require attention periodically in order to keep them in satisfactory condition. Ordinary use results in wear and tear, making cleaning, oiling, adjusting, and installing new parts the rule rather than the exception. Preventive maintenance, rather than remedial maintenance, should be stressed. The former seeks to catch trouble before it happens; this is accomplished by scheduling inspections at carefully determined intervals. The latter, or remedial maintenance, deals with trouble after it occurs. Preventive maintenance provides greater employee satisfaction and efficient product performance. Uninterrupted service at the lowest cost should be the chief objective. Maintenance can be handled in any of four ways: maintenance contracts, individual service calls, company-operated service, and combined leasing-maintenance contracts.

Many manufacturers, or their sales distributors, prefer to service their products in order to insure complete satisfaction; and to this end, they offer maintenance contracts which call for regular inspection, cleaning, adjusting, and oiling. Charges are made on a predetermined basis, and the rates and conditions for special service calls are usually stated. Advocates of this type of maintenance service claim that the regularity of service, the use of genuine parts, the employment of skilled, factory-trained mechanics, and the overall, long-range low cost warrant its use. This means is probably the most popular for offices of all sizes.

Individual service calls are a "when required" type of service. This is sometimes called "no service contract" maintenance. It is of a remedial nature. The age and number of units are the chief factors which influence the choice of this policy. If most of the units are new, it is reasonable to expect that they will not require repair service; likewise, when a large number are in use, it is logical that not all will require maintenance service. However, a service call on an individual basis usually costs more than one under a maintenance contract. Also, the regular cleaning and oiling of most equipment and machines are usually advisable, and these must be provided on an individual service basis when this plan of maintenance is used.

A company-operated service is followed primarily because of considerations of cost, control, or availability of service. Maintenance costs may be lower under this plan, provided there is a sufficient volume to warrant full-time maintenance employees. With a company-operated service, it is possible to exercise close control over the progress of the work, the expenses, and the regularity of inspections. In some instances, available outside services are inconvenient, owing to the remoteness of the office, and in such cases the company-operated plan may be desirable.

When a facility is leased, the leasor usually provides for the maintenance. Terms for such service are included in the lease. Both periodic and on-call maintenance are provided. Also, as a part of the agreement any design improvements in the unit or its attachments are usually supplied as quickly as available.

OFFICE CHAIRS

Knowledge of available office equipment and machines is essential in automation. In this connection we normally think of machines only, but information on equipment is also important because it is essential to the total processing picture. The first equipment facility to be discussed is office chairs.

The office chair is probably the most important physical facility in an office. It is personal to the employee and vitally affects the ease and comfort with which the work is done. Most office work is of a sedentary nature, a fact which further stresses the importance of the office chair. among the many types of office chairs are the familiar straight-back chair, the swivel chair, chairs that tilt, the posture chair, plain or upholstered chairs, wood or metal chairs, and chairs with or without armrests. Certain features about chairs require careful consideration by the office manager. Upholstering generally adds to appearance and comfort; but it requires periodic cleaning and, in the case of leather, "dressing" in order to preserve the material. Caster wheels made from relatively hard material are usually best for use on carpeting, while casters of softer material should be used on composition tile and wood flooring.

In the office, posture chairs are very important. The chair has three adjustments, thereby making it possible to "tailor-fit" the chair to the occupant. These adjustments include:

1. *The seat height*—so that the feet are comfortably placed on the floor and no undue pressure is present on the underside of the leg just above the knee.

2. *The backrest height*—so that support is provided the small or lumbar region of the back. The swivel joint of the backrest should be approximately one inch higher than the top of the hip bone.

3. *The backrest horizontal position*—so that the muscles covering the two pelvic bones, i.e., the glutei muscles, overhang slightly the rear edge of the seat, thus placing the body weight forward on the underside of the leg muscles.

Even though available, these adjustments are frequently not used, thus incorrect seating exists as illustrated by Figure 25.

The major consideration about a posture chair is that it be used properly. Simply supplying a posture chair seldom assures that the benefits of good posture seating are being enjoyed. The occupant must know how to sit in the chair and must sit that way. The proper use of posture chairs improves the appearance of office employees, reduces fatigue, improves morale, and aids in the functioning of important body actions, including breathing, circulation, and elimination.

OFFICE DESKS

An office desk provides a work surface, a temporary storage for materials being processed, and a convenient area for selected tools and machines required in accomplishing the work. The trend in desk appearance is toward smooth, streamlined surfaces. Supports touching the floor are recessed in order to conceal them from view, to permit ample toe room when standing near the desk, and to facilitate cleaning the floor. Steel desks are equipped with linoleum or plastic; lighter colors and finishes seem to be preferred. Many wood desks are finished with light stain and bleached colors. Hardware and exposed metal parts are of dull finish to avoid annoying highlights.

Chair Too High
Seat pressures nerves and stops circulation just above the knee.

Chair Too Low
Steady pressure on spine causes great fatigue.

Chair Back Too High
No needed support to spine, causing slumping and a strain on back and shoulder muscles.

Chair Tilts Back Too Far
Occupant easily gets off balance, with excessive back strain.

FIG. 25.   Examples of common incorrect seating.

Further comments about desks will be centered around desk efficiency, design, and dimensions.

1. *Desk efficiency.*   A desk is actually a basic working tool, and this should be kept in mind when planning. Viewing a desk as a working tool emphasizes the meaning of desk efficiency, which is influenced by (1) the design features of the desk and (2) the person using the desk. The former stresses the old adage: "A place for everything, and everything in its place." The desk and its interior are planned to give maximum service to the user. Tailor-made desk-drawer arrangements are available to aid work production. As new requirements arise, the drawers can be interchanged and rearranged as desired. Figure 26 suggests efficient arrangement of materials in desk drawers to meet specific requirements.

The second factor—the person using the desk—emphasizes the influence of the desk user's work habits and attitudes upon desk efficiency. The personnel element is vital and necessitates adequate instructions, training, and supervising. To assist in achieving desk efficiency, the following guides are listed:

1. Work on one task at a time and finish it before starting another. Abstain from trying to do several tasks at the same time.

2. Keep the desk free from excess papers and supplies. Have only those items on the desk that are needed. The desk top is a work surface and should facilitate immediate action.

3. Shelve material that is not urgent. For example, insert slips in magazines to articles to be read and then put them to one side for reading in off moments.

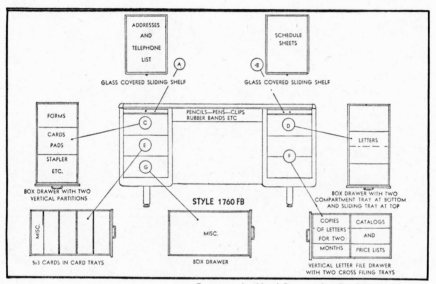

Courtesy: Art Metal Construction Co., Jamestown, N.Y.

FIG. 26.   Suggested desk-drawer layout to meet individual requirements for order department manager.

4. Strive to keep the work moving over the desk. Take action on each paper coming to the desk as quickly as possible.

5. Act on important paper work first. Have a daily schedule, and make use of a desk calendar to guide the sequence of work.

6. Dispose of all mail before going home. Do not permit a stack of mixed-up papers to remain overnight and cause a poor start the next day.

2. Desk design. Desks are designed to serve particular needs. Among the most popular are those for executives, junior executives, stenographers, typists, adding and calculating machine operators, and billing clerks. Desks are available in single- and double-pedestal styles. The pedestal is the support or foundation of the desk, and it contains the drawers or a foldaway platform which houses a typewriter or some special machine. The single-pedestal desk is used in cases where a single tier of desk drawers and a smaller-size top are sufficient. Figure 27 illustrates several different types of desks designed to serve particular requirements.

Courtesy: Art Metal Construction Co., Jamestown, N.Y.

FIG. 27.   This office features desks designed to meet specific work requirements. Observe in the foreground the fixed-bed typewriter desk; in the left background, the general-purpose desk; and in the right background, the desk with an overhang top.

Especially where an electric typewriter is used, a great many companies have adopted the machine platform arrangement in conjunction with the ordinary desk. Figure 28 shows such an arrangement. The platform can be attached to either side of the desk. Economy and efficiency are gained. Provided is a firmer base than the disappearing platform, more knee space, and desk drawers for supplies.

The "conference desk" has an oversized top that overhangs the pedestals at one or both ends and at the back. At meetings, it is possible for five or six people to sit comfortably around a conference desk, since ample work space and leg room are provided. The conference desk has become quite popular; it adds prestige to an executive's office. An attractive functional desk featuring modern design is shown in Figure 29.

3. *Desk dimensions.* Dimensions of desks vary with the type of desk, the material used, and the manufacturer. Executive desks are usually the largest, sizes ranging from 76 x 36 inches to 60 x 32 inches being the most common. For general office work, sizes from 60 x 34 inches to 42 x 30 inches are popular. The trend is toward smaller desks. For example, most new general office desks are 50 to 55 inches wide instead of the former 60 inches, and 30 inches deep instead of 34 inches. In some companies,

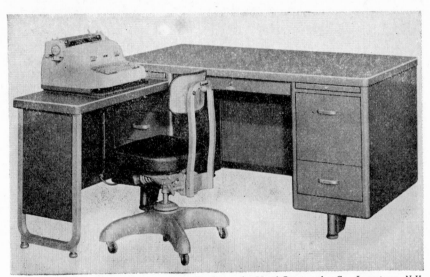

Courtesy: Art Metal Construction Co., Jamestown, N.Y.

FIG. 28. A machine platform attached to a steel office desk.

however, certain sizes are specified for certain uses. For example, in one company, the following applies:

Employee	Desk-Top Size
Department head	78 x 38 inches, triple overhang
Supervisor	60 x 36 inches, front overhang
Staff	60 x 30 inches or special-purpose desk
Clerical	60 x 30 inches

Desks are made of various heights. Currently the preferred height is 28½ or 29 inches. It is claimed that for the average employee this height is better since it helps to maximize the employee's comfort.

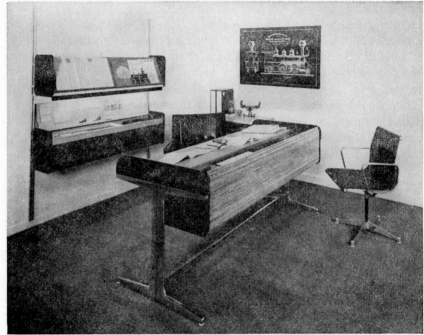

Courtesy: Herman Miller, Inc., Zeeland, Mich.

FIG. 29.   A functional desk featuring modern design.

MODULAR OFFICE FURNITURE

This type of furniture consists of easily and quickly assembled modular components which, when assembled, comprise an effective functional and modern arrangement. Basic units include such "building blocks" as desk tops, desk pedestals, auxiliary tops, end supports, and filing and shelving units. In a number of installations, modular components have been put together to form a U-shaped desk and platform arrangement as illustrated by Figure 30. Partition panels for privacy can be added to meet individual requirements. Components are standard and interchangeable, thus supplying flexibility and many various combinations.

POSTING-TRAY UNIT

This equipment is commonly used in connection with machine installations and is designed to provide convenient reference to sheets or cards. Rapid removal and return of the material, quick access to accounts, locking in sheets to prevent unauthorized removal, clear vision, and a

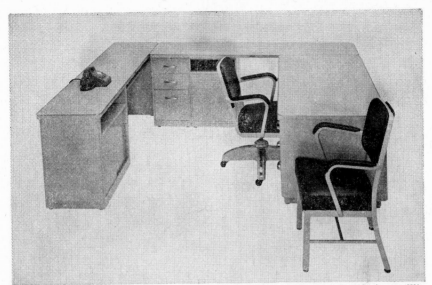

Courtesy: Invincible Metal Furniture Co., Manitowoc, Wis.

FIG. 30.   Modular office components assembled to provide an efficient U-shaped unit.

clean, orderly arrangement of records are among the features of this posting unit. Illustrations are shown in Figure 31.

PUNCHED-CARD MACHINES

Among the most important and versatile of all office machines are punched-card machines which put information in such a form that it can be easily handled for any of a number of subsequent operations. The "punched card" is the key physical unit about which the whole process revolves. The common language supplied by this card provides the real significance to these machines.[2] They provide flexibility, accuracy, and rapidity to data processing and are employed for many different uses, including the analyzing and summarizing of statistical data, the writing of invoices, payrolls, inventory control, labor distribution, market research, sales reports, and accounts payable. They are also used to obtain correlated data. In market research studies, for example, the number of respondents who answered "Yes" to a given question, broken down according to age, income, and occupation, can be quickly obtained. Likewise, sales analyses by units, dollars, territories, and months, or

---

[2] Punched cards as a medium for data processing are discussed in Chapters 6 and 7.

Courtesy: LeFebure Corp., Cedar Rapids, Iowa

FIG. 31. (*Left*) Posting-tray equipment adjustable in height from 31¼ inches for standing position to 22 inches for seated position. (*Right*) The specially designed tray expedites the posting.

manufacturing costs by various types of labor operations, can be easily determined.

ARRANGEMENT OF DATA ON CARD

Holes are coded to represent either alphabetical or numerical information. For example, vertical columns of the card are allocated to different items. Information on months is given two columns so that a 1 in the first column and a 0 in the second is punched to indicate 10, or the month of October. The IBM card has 80 columns, the RR card has 90 columns, hence a maximum of 80 or 90 letters or numbers per card is permitted. Figure 32 shows the allocation of space on a punched card covering accounts receivable. In this illustration, the number 1 punched out in each of the first two columns indicates the eleventh month, or November. The code followed for punched holes is given in Chapter 7.

Laying out the punched card or deciding what information to punch in the card warrants careful thought. This emphasizes the planning function. Only information which is valuable to management, which will reveal pertinent major relationships, and which will provide the basis for meaningful subanalyses should be included.

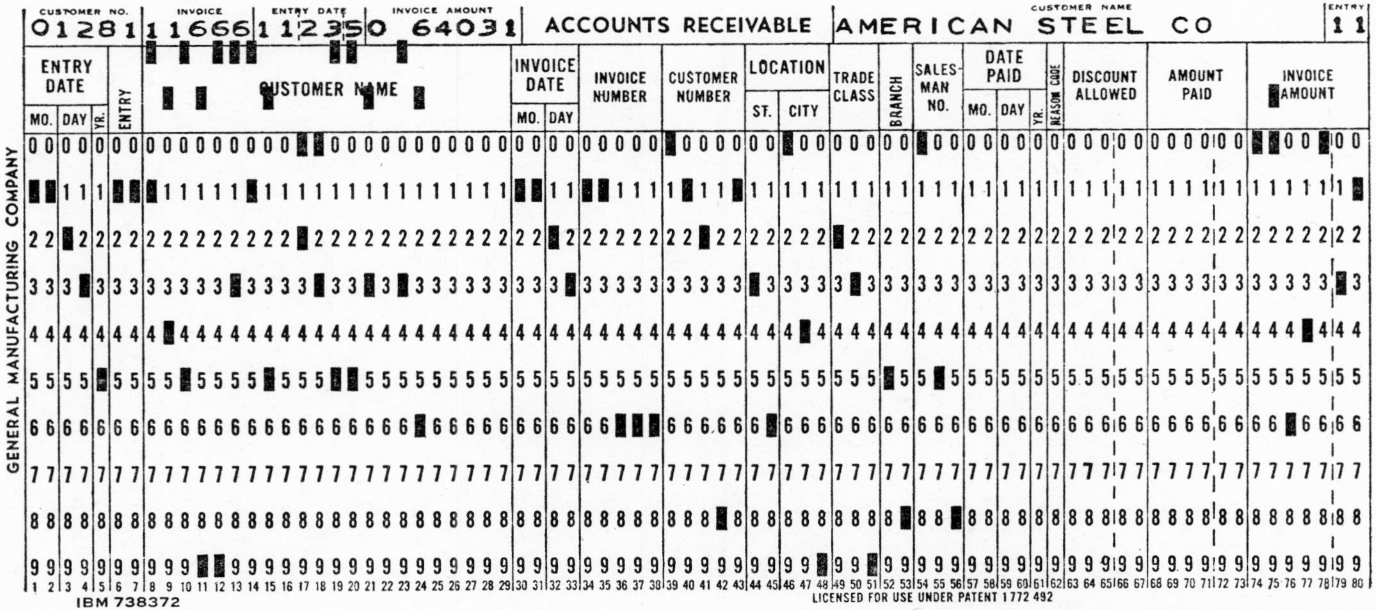

FIG. 32. The space on the punched card is allocated according to the needs of the particular study.

Courtesy: International Business Machines Corp., New York

BASIC PUNCHED-CARD MACHINES

There are three basic punched-card machines, including a punching machine, a sorter, and a tabulator. A punching machine punches small holes in the card, representing the numerical and alphabetical information desired. The machines have many automatic features, depending upon the model and the manufacturer. Figure 33 shows a card-punching machine.

The sorter arranges the cards according to any desired classification and in alphabetical or numerical sequence. The sorting is really a box sort. Cards are passed through the machine; and the punched hole causes a mechanism to operate, resulting in the card being directed into a specific box or pocket of the machine. Sorting at any one time is done according to one vertical column, i.e., a unit number or a letter. For example, consider the numbers in the left column of Figure 34 as the data to be placed in proper numerical sequence. The first sort arranges the data in sequence according to the unit column. Then, the second sort rearranges this sequence according to the 10's column. In like manner, the third sort rearranges the 100's column, thus placing the cards in proper numerical sequence. Sorting machines are capable of handling 1,000 cards per minute, or 60,000 per hour.

The tabulator prepares printed reports from the data contained on the punched and sorted cards. These machines can print individually or in summary; a great variety of reports is possible. The number of reports that can be printed is almost limitless but depends mainly upon the information to be "read" by the

Courtesy: International Business Machines Corp., New York

FIG. 33. A card-punching machine which features an automatic card control of skipping and duplicating, a fast method of duplication when desired, and a design which permits efficient and rapid operation.

machine, the forms on which the reports are prepared, and the arrangement and rearrangement of the cards. A tabulator—or as it is sometimes called, a punched-card accounting machine—is illustrated in Figure 35.

Unsorted Data	Arrangement after First Sort	Arrangement after Second Sort	Arrangement after Third Sort
	↓	↓	↓
828....................	750	904	107
107....................	460	107	191
542....................	191	212	212
904....................	542	828	375
212....................	212	542	388
375....................	904	750	460
191....................	375	460	542
750....................	107	375	750
388....................	828	388	828
460....................	388	191	904

FIG. 34.

Courtesy: International Business Machines Corp., New York

FIG. 35. A punched-card accounting machine that provides an economic and rapid method of printing from punched cards.

SPECIAL PUNCHED-CARD MACHINES

Special machines for specific operations are also available. A complete listing of these is beyond the scope of this discussion, but the more common ones will be included. A machine called an "interpreter" prints at the top of the card the data represented by the punched holes. This information is sometimes desired for quick identification and reference. However, many experienced and skilled operators can read the punched cards as easily as the average person reads normal print. A "verifier" can be used to check the accuracy of the holes punched in the cards. Another machine, called a reproducer or "gang punch," is designed to punch standardized information on cards. For example, data such as date and location of customer, which are repetitive for a batch of cards, can be punched at one time and not performed individually for each card. There is also a calculator, or "multiplying punch," which senses, for example, two factors prepunched in the card, computes the product, punches it into the card, and records the factors and the product on a paper.

Variable information such as meter readings, job data, and stores requisitions can be pencil-marked in appropriate spaces on a punched-card area. Then, by means of a machine called an "optical scanning punch," the variable information is read and automatically punched into the card, thus making it ready for processing.

With the developments in office automation and especially source data automation, many punched cards are now produced simultaneously with the typing of the information on a typewriter equipped with special attachments or units "connected with" the typewriter. Such machines are discussed in the following chapter.

USAGE OF PUNCHED CARD MACHINES

The most common uses for punched-card machines are (1) correlating, analyzing, and summarizing data, such as sales by customer, and net revenue by salesman, as illustrated by Figure 36; (2) preparing bills or invoices—the data on cards can be easily grouped and totaled; (3) handling accounts payable—each payment to a creditor is processed via a punched card; (4) keeping inventory records—purchases and usages by items are simple operations with punched cards; (5) preparing payrolls and distributing labor costs—checks are prepared from information on the card for each employee, and tabular lists can be quickly run as well as labor cost allocated to predetermined groups; and (6) production control— for each production operation, pertinent data and its relationship to other operations are put on separate punched cards, from which production routing and dispatching information are easily prepared.

Key considerations in the usage of punched cards include the cost and time of getting the raw data punched into the cards, the extent to which correlated or listed information will be helpful, and the value of additional facts gained from being able to interpret the data in a more feasible form.

SALES AND GROSS PROFIT BY CUSTOMER

CUSTOMER		COMMODITY		QUANTITY	UNIT	COST OF GOODS SOLD	SALES AMOUNT
BR.	NO.	CODE	DESCRIPTION				
1 3	6 7		A C E D R U G C O				
1 3	6 7	0 3 0 1	B E A U T Y S O A P R E G U L A R	1 2	D Z	1 9¦8 0	2 4¦0 0
1 3	6 7	0 3 0 2	B E A U T Y S O A P G U E S T	1 2	D Z	2 0¦4 0	2 5¦2 0
1 3	6 7	0 3 0 3	B E A U T Y S O A P B A T H	1 2	D Z	2 1¦6 0	2 7¦0 0
1 3	6 7	1 3 1 4	S H A V E S O A P L A R G E	2 4	D Z	4 8¦0 0	6 9¦6 0
1 3	6 7	1 3 5 2	B R U S H L E S S C R E A M L R G	2 4	D Z	3 1¦2 0	4 3¦2 0
			[FOR THE PURPOSE OF THIS EXHIBIT, ONLY] [A FEW COMMODITIES ARE ILLUSTRATED]				
						2 7 5¦0 0 ✻	3 7 5¦0 0
1 3	1 0 5		A D A M S D R Y G O O D S C O				
1 3	1 0 5	0 3 0 1	B E A U T Y S O A P R E G U L A R	2 4	D Z	3 9¦6 0	4 8¦0 0

NET REVENUE ANALYSIS BY SALESMAN

BRANCH	SALESMAN		GROSS SALES	RETURNS AND ALLOWANCES	NET SALES	COST SALES	TRAVEL AND EXPENSE	COM
	NO.	NAME						
1 3	2 9	A ANDREWS	5 4 0 3¦0 0	3 7 5¦0 0	5 0 2 8¦0 0	2 9 6 0¦0 0	2 5¦7 0	
1 3	3 2	G DRISCOLL	6 1 1 9¦0 0	4 3 5¦0 0	5 6 8 4¦0 0	3 8 2 5¦0 0	2 6¦4 0	
1 3	4 5	R M EDWARDS	3 9 0 5¦0 0	3 4 0¦0 0	3 5 6 5¦0 0	2 2 4 0¦0 0	2 9¦0 0	
1 3	4 7	A H FRANKLIN	7 5 1 3¦0 0	4 5 0¦0 0	7 0 6 3¦0 0	5 1 3 5¦0 0	2 8¦0 0	
1 3	5 1	J A HOLLAND	6 2 5 7¦0 0	4 4 1¦0 0	5 8 1 6¦0 0	3 8 5 5¦0 0	2 6¦2 5	
1 3	5 5	L B LAWSON	6 1 2 0¦0 0	4 2 9¦0 0	5 6 9 1¦0 0	3 8 5 0¦0 0	2 5¦7 5	

Courtesy: International Business Machines Corp., New York

FIG. 36. Samples of the work prepared by a tabulator of punched cards.

The use of punched cards is not necessarily confined to large companies. In most instances, punched cards are feasible when the data (1) are fairly repetitious, permitting prepunching for much of the data, and (2) require analysis to show pertinent relationships.

MARGINAL NOTCHED-CARD MACHINES

These machines are used to notch precoded holes *along the edge* of a card so that sorting of the data by key classifications can be accomplished quickly and accurately. After sorting, data referring to a similar attribute, such as sales, inventories, or indirect labor costs, can be totaled and used in management reports. The process is versatile; it is applicable to many transactions, including sales orders, stock requisitions, purchase and expense vouchers, payroll records, and production control data.

The cards are available in varying sizes; for example, there are 2 x 3½-inch and 7½ x 8½-inch cards. Pertinent information is written in the center position of the card. Holes along the margins are assigned definite values depending upon their location. Identification with a particular classification is made by notching away the portion of the card between the hole and the edge. For example, in Figure 37, the operation number 24 can be identified by the notches in the upper left margin of the card where the 2 under the 10's and the 4 under the units have been notched. Likewise, the date, May 22, is coded in the left margin, indicating that the month is 5 and the day is 22. Observe that for any one segment, the holes of values 7,

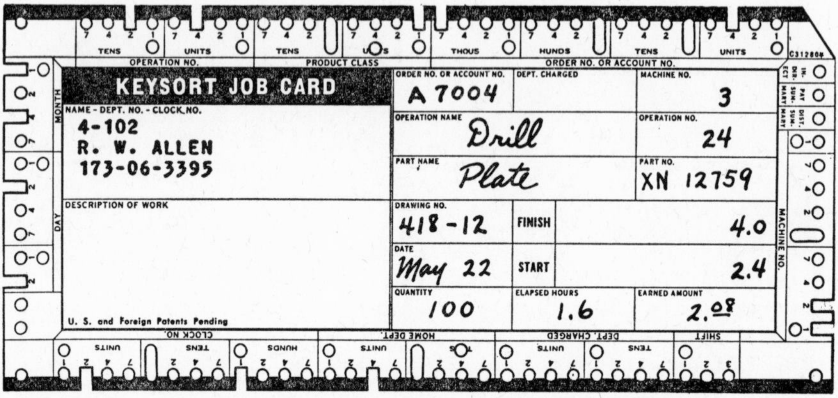

Courtesy: Royal-McBee Corp., New York

FIG. 37.   Card punched with holes and notches to indicate definite information.

4, 2, and 1 make possible any value from 1 through 9. Zero is indicated by no notches.

To sort cards, either a special machine or a manual means can be used. The former is recommended for large volumes of cards. The latter utilizes a single or a multiprong fork which is positioned so that it slides through a designated hole or holes in a stack of cards. By shaking the pack, the operator causes the cards with notched holes at the prong location to fall clear of the other cards. In this way a fast, accurate sort is provided.

ACCOUNTING MACHINES

In this category we include billing machines, posting machines, and bookkeeping machines. These machines are basically mechanical aids which simplify and expedite paper work. Many are equipped with "bars," or accumulating registers, which make it possible to summarize and to distribute accounts, a valuable feature particularly with records dealing with cost, sales, and payroll. These machines are not wholly automatic. Usually the proper keys must be depressed and the motor bar pushed to start each cycle of machine operation. Some are equipped with a calculating mechanism for multiplying and adding from which the operator reads the calculated amount and types it in the appropriate column. Many feature checking or proofing devices the designs of which

Basis of Classification	Types	
Keyboard....	*Descriptive Machine.* Equipped with both typewriter and numerical keyboards.	*Nondescriptive Machine.* Has numerical keyboard only.
Bed..........	*Flat Bed Machine.* The printing surface and the papers are placed horizontally onto this flat bed. Advocates claim it simplifies insertion of papers.	*Platen or Carriage Machine.* The papers are inserted in the carriage, and platen is turned similar to that of a typewriter.
Print........	*Single-Print Machine.* Prints two or more copies simultaneously. Papers are inserted into machine as a pack with carbon interleaved.	*Multiprint Machine.* Papers are placed side by side into the machine, which prints one paper and then moves over and prints the same data or portions of them on the other paper.
Style........	*Window Machine.* Papers are placed in an opening or window; machine entries are printed while papers are held in this position. Easily handles entries in booklets, as in a bank, and expedites visual checking by operator and customers.	*Nonwindow Machine.* Papers are placed in the carriage or on the flat bed—there is no window opening of the machine.

FIG. 38. Common classifications of accounting machines.

differ with different manufacturers. In some, they consist of showing a number which is compared with an original, such as "old balance," or with an entry number, for proof of accuracy. For each horizontal line of figures, the proof-line figure must be equal to that of the old balance; otherwise, an error is in that horizontal line. In some cases, the machine locks and will not print if old entries have been picked up incorrectly. Accounting machines can be classified in a number of ways. Figure 38 shows some common bases for classifying machines, along with comments on each type of machine.

DESCRIPTIVE ACCOUNTING MACHINE

To illustrate further the types of accounting machines and the kind of work done with them, several brief descriptions will be included. The first is the descriptive accounting machine, for which the work of accounts payable can be used. For illustrative purposes, the work of a purchase journal, remittance advice, and distribution expense ledger are used. These are shown by Figure 39. These data are printed simultaneously by the descriptive accounting machine. The machine's typewriter is used to write in the descriptive material of the vendors' names on the purchase journal. For example, referring to Figure 39, the purchases from Smith Supply Company are posted January 9, for $16 and $8.50, making the balance due $170. For inventory or expense purposes, the items are distributed directly to the proper column, shown in the upper right of the figure. The item for $16 is charged to Miscellaneous account 84; and likewise, the second item of $8.50 is charged to Miscellaneous account 92. These data are printed on the respective distribution ledgers, as shown by the illustration. Distribution totals are accumulated automatically. The same machine can be used if a voucher check is used instead of a remittance advice. When due, the remittance advice is paid, less any discount allowed. Illustration of this work is not included here; but for this payment work, a check and a check register are prepared simultaneously by the same machine. A carbon copy of the check is made on the office copy of the remittance notice. Partial payments are handled by posting to suppliers' accounts during the check-writing operation. Checks written that do not affect accounts payable, such as those to replenish the petty cash fund or for transportation charges, are written and distributed directly to the columns affected.

Different features are stressed by different descriptive accounting machines. Most are adaptable for many different types of work and are useful for any one or all types, including general ledger, accounts payable, accounts receivable, and payroll. Figure 40 shows a popular model. This machine features a single keyboard, program keys on the typewriter, and an electronic processing unit housed in the pedestal of the desklike unit. For the work of billing, the operator has only to enter figures and descriptions, and the machine automatically does the rest, including extensions, additions, deductions, percentages, discounts, subtractions, and totals. The machine automatically handles calculations in quantities of dozens and pieces, decimals, fractions, and for use in the lumber industry converts board feet into square feet and accumulates the number of pieces of lumber and the linear feet.

NONDESCRIPTIVE ACCOUNTING MACHINE

Figure 41 shows a nondescriptive accounting machine. In discussing the work of this type of accounting machine, sometimes referred to as a numerical keyboard accounting machine, consider accounts receivable work in which the ledger, statement, and proof-tape journal are prepared. Figure 42 shows these records. To illustrate, for the last entry, the

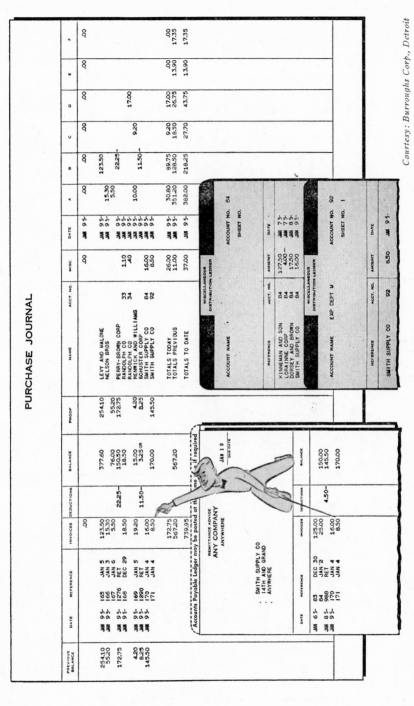

FIG. 39. Remittance advice, purchase journal with distribution, and distribution ledger prepared simultaneously with a descriptive accounting machine.

Courtesy: Burroughs Corp., Detroit

Courtesy: Friden, Inc., San Leandro, Calif.

FIG. 40. The 5010 COMPUTYPER Electronic Billing/ Accounting Machine produces completed invoices at electronic speeds. Data are stored, calculations performed in milliseconds, and removal program panels are featured for unlimited machine applications.

Courtesy: Burroughs Corp., Detroit

FIG. 41. A modern nondescriptive accounting machine.

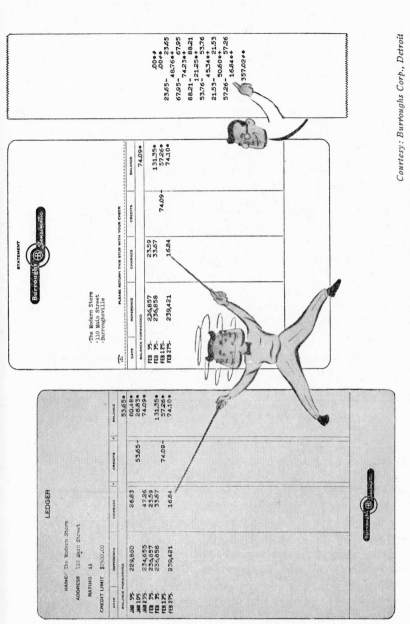

Courtesy: Burroughs Corp., Detroit

FIG. 42. Accounts receivable work consisting of original ledger, statement, and proof-tape journal. The entries are made by the machine shown in Figure 41.

operator inserted the forms into the machine; entered the old balance, the reference numbers, and the charge by depressing the proper keys; then actuated the machine by the motor bar. The machine automatically prints all the needed information, including date, reference number, charges, and the new balance, on the three forms. To reset the machine for other accounting forms, such as accounts payable, a quick adjustment is provided by turning a knob at either side of the machine. The letter material at the top of the ledger and the statement can be written by means of a typewriter or an addressing machine. The ledger copy is permanent and retained; a statement is mailed monthly to the customer.

WINDOW-POSTING ACCOUNTING MACHINE

The window-posting cash register type of accounting machine, sometimes referred to as a "teller's machine," is different in operation and appearance from the majority of others and is especially adapted to use by retail stores, banks, and hotels. With this type of machine, the payment of a bill or a deposit in a bank is handled by inserting the customer's ledger card and statement or book into the machine. The proper keys are depressed; and when the machine is actuated, the entries are printed on the inserted forms and also on a machine audit sheet or roll which shows the total transactions. The necessary calculations are then made automatically by the machine, and the new balances are printed on the forms. A window-posting cash register accounting machine is illustrated by Figure 43.

ADDRESSING AND LISTING MACHINES

Affixing addresses or other information in applications where the same information is used periodically typifies one of the popular uses for addressing and listing machines. Their widest application is probably in addressing envelopes or advertising literature. The use of these machines is beneficial wherever a small quantity of identical information must be written repeatedly. In addition to mailing lists, the following are typical applications: names of employees along with standardized payroll information, i.e., check number and social security number; addresses on shipping labels and tags; headings on invoices and ledger cards; listing of customers; items ordered; items of storekeeping; lists of tools; tax roll; names and addresses of stockholders; and the list of dividend recipients.

There are two types of addressing and listing machines: those using metal-embossed plates and those using fiber or tissue stencils. Metal plates are made in a machine especially designed for that purpose. The plate is

Courtesy: National Cash Register Co., Dayton

FIG. 43. A window-posting cash register type of accounting machine.

stamped, thus forcing the required impressions in the metal. Metal plates give very long service; they practically never wear out. The fiber stencils can be prepared on a typewriter equipped with a special platen, last a long time, but should be handled carefully. It is also possible to type or cut a punched tape which, when fed through an automatic machine for making plates, will produce them at a high rate of speed.

Most machines using metal plates permit attachments which add considerably to their value for specific operations. Included are:

1. *A cutoff device.* This permits only part of the plate to print at one time. It is useful where a portion of the information on the plate is printed in the first column of a spread sheet, another part in the second column, a third part in a third column, and so on.

2. *A selector.* By its use certain plates pass through the machine without writing. This feature is desirable, for example, when certain plates are wanted for a particular mailing. The sequence of the plates remains unchanged.

3. *A repeater.* Duplicate impressions are made from each plate before advancing to the next plate. To illustrate, the name and address might be required on the check stub and on the check, or on the statement and on the envelope. Settings for triplicate impressions are also available.

4. *A dating device.* This enters the date simultaneously with the printing of other data. It is used in connection with statements and letters.

5. *Tabbing sockets.* By inserting small metal projections into selected tabs of the plate, selective sorting of the plates is accomplished. The sockets are located along the top edge of the plate and tabs are inserted according to a code.

MISCELLANEOUS EQUIPMENT AND MACHINES

Numbering devices are used to place numbers chronologically on incoming orders, memorandums, and other papers in order to process the papers more effectively. They are offered in a variety of sizes, capacities, and prices. Well designed, they give satisfactory service for many years.

Check protectors are employed to make out checks in perforated print so that the chances for altering the words or figures are eliminated. Different styles and types of print are available. Most check protectors are manually operated. Also offered are units that sign checks, thus eliminating much laborious and repetitious work for some executives.

Copyholders, especially helpful for stenographers doing copy work, hold papers in place at a convenient reading level. A horizontal bar guides the eye to the proper line. Since the material is held in a proper reading position, posture is aided and eyestrain, head twisting, and fatiguing refocusing of the eyes are eliminated.

A time punch prepares cards by punching the start and stop times directly into the card. The punched cards can be processed immediately and no manual computation of elapsed time or verification are required. The machine is used for labor cost analysis, production control, and machine loading. Figure 44 shows this machine.

Counters provide quick measurement of units and the speed of certain office work. Bank checks, cards, and labels, for example, can be quickly counted by use of these machines. Some are operated manually, while others are attached to common office machines to indicate such information as the number of strokes of typing

Courtesy: Universal Time Punch, Inc., Cleveland

FIG. 44. A time-punch machine that records time records by punching directly a tab or time card.

on a typewriter or the revolutions of the cylindrical drum of a duplicating machine.

Labeling machines prepare addressed labels in long, continuous-length strips. The back of the labels is mucilaged. The strips are cut automatically and individually for each label just prior to its being affixed to an envelope, package, or periodical. The labels are available in a variety of sizes. The speed of the machine is relatively high.

Electric staplers, used for attaching sheets of paper together, are employed for large volumes of this work. The stapling of booklets or reports, for example, is illustrative. Savings of much effort and time are gained by using an electric stapler.

CHAPTER SIX

SOURCE DATA

AUTOMATION

Nature gave men two ends—one to sit on and one to think with. Ever since then man's success or failure has been dependent on the one he used most.
—George R. Kirkpatrick

As POINTED out in Chapter 1, source data automation (SDA) is a major part of the current office technology. The identification of SDA is given to data processing that primarily, but not exclusively, ties together various types of office machines by common media and integrates their respective operations so as to form a whole from the various machines utilized. Computers can be included but they are not a mandatory part of SDA data-processing equipment.

IDENTIFICATION AND EVOLUTION OF SDA

In the processing of business data, it is customary to find certain data copied and repeated over and over again, rearranged according to many different formats, and originated in or sent to different locations. In addition, business data are interrelated. For example, data showing price figures alone mean little. Required, in addition to price, are vendor's name, address, and terms of sale. Likewise, a single figure showing the quantity of an item on hand is insufficient. The units of measurement, location, cost, and source may also be necessary.

Consider the paper work required to handle a customer's order. Raw materials must be purchased or, if stocked, the inventory records consulted, release orders to manufacture issued, production-scheduled shipping tickets and bills of lading prepared, and invoices made out to the customer. Much of the information used in preparing these various documents is similar, and the data are written many times. Distribution of the information may be made to a considerable number of locations, some of which are miles apart, as, for example, a branch factory and the central office building.

It is logical to attempt to simplify and integrate the writing of these various office forms. The elimination of duplicate writings can be accomplished by using carbon copies; an accounting machine extends and totals; and information punched in code on cards can be used repeatedly to reproduce all documents required. But in general, these deal with a single process and are not interchangeable among various processes. However, in some instances, as in duplicating copies containing essential information for specific purposes, such as purchasing or production control, the copies serve in several processes, and all the writing is integrated by use of the one master.

The name, source data automation, is self-explanatory. It is the automation of source data—where information begins. Full benefits of automation are thus acquired because the automation applies to the entire range of the data-processing system, not to just the end-product areas. Data recorded are in effect self-perpetuating and can be used over and over for as many times as is necessary to satisfy the varied requirements. To illustrate, the writing for an office operation is put into such a form that subsequent operations requiring this writing can be processed automatically. SDA therefore tends to tie office work together, to integrate it, or to form a whole from the various parts. Mechanization is used. In fact, SDA can be viewed as integrating common machines which are basically dissimilar into a purposeful, coordinated mechanized group.

SDA was introduced in 1954 by executives of the U.S Steel Corporation. They used it for various portions of their paper work operations. Employing the medium of punched cards and perforated tapes, the original data were transferred to one of these media and subsequently processed on any of several common machines. Those work portions which were different for each processing were performed manually, but a large percentage of the total work was automated.

The idea was quickly exploited by many other companies. Some viewed it as a means for utilizing common office machines more effectively, others as an economical way to integrate data, and still others as a way to employ their computers economically and to extend their field of application. Within a short period, "common language" machines or attachments to common machines became readily available. The vast array of equipment, including card-reading machines, paper-tape reading machines, and optical-character recognition machines, made it feasible to keep alive data without the need for direct manual rehandling.

THE COMMON LANGUAGE LINK

To implement SDA, conventional office machines must be adapted to speak the same language; that is, a basic and direct compatibility, so to speak, between different types of machines, and between machines of different manufacturers, must be achieved. In this manner, data originating on one type of machine can be used later on other types, without human reading, interpreting, and writing.

The common language medium joining all machines utilized is the key to the mechanization aspect of source data automation. The medium is acceptable to all the machines, permits each to perform its particular task, passes the result on to the next machine, which utilizes this information and passes on the accumulated data. In essence, the group of conventional

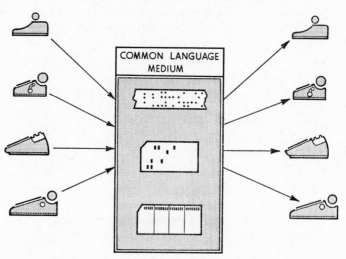

FIG. 45.   The key to SDA is the common language medium integrating the common office machines.

machines is connected into a harmonious entirety. When the machines are widely dispersed geographically, appropriate media are available for the necessary communication. The idea of the common language link in SDA is shown graphically by Figure 45.

There are three common language media in use today: (1) perforated tape, (2) punched card, and (3) edge-punched card. Whatever the medium, it is prepared simultaneously with the initial writing of the data. To reiterate, when a sales order is initially typed, a mechanism attached to the typewriter automatically prepares the medium. As stated above, this medium is then used to operate all subsequent machines required.

Normally, each machine is equipped either to prepare the medium or to "read" it, or both. Figure 46 illustrates a nondescriptive accounting machine connected to a tape perforator. In this application, the following is performed in one operation: A voucher is posted, the voucher check is computed and printed, and a voucher register is prepared. Integrated with this operation, a perforated tape is made for subsequent preparation of punched cards used in the processing and the analyzing of the data.

One widely used perforated tape has five rows or channels of perforations. Various combinations of holes in these five channels give a total of 32 symbols, including the 26-letter alphabet, letters, figures, space, carriage

Courtesy: Burroughs Corp., Detroit

FIG. 46. Installation of an accounting machine connected to tape perforator providing perforated tape for subsequent integrated data processing.

return, line feed, and blank. A shift symbol provides for numerals. Figure 47 shows the five-channel code for perforated tape.

It must not be concluded that perforated tape is limited to five channels. Actually, up to eight channels can be used; this permits more characters and check and control symbols. A seven-channel tape, for example, would require all equipment using this tape to be so equipped for it. As long as the operations are within an enterprise, no particular difficulty would be present; but in dealing with outside firms, difficulty would be encountered if they use tape of a different number of channels.

Punched cards are also a medium for conveying data in an SDA arrangement. The data are put into punched cards which serve to operate all subsequent machines in the process. Historically, this was the first medium used.

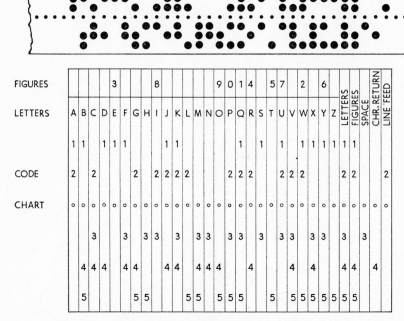

	A	B	C	D	E	F	G	H	I	J	K	L	M	N	O	P	Q	R	S	T	U	V	W	X	Y	Z	LETTERS	FIGURES	SPACE	CHR. RETURN	LINE FEED
FIGURES					3				8						9	0	1	4		5	7		2		6						
LETTERS	A	B	C	D	E	F	G	H	I	J	K	L	M	N	O	P	Q	R	S	T	U	V	W	X	Y	Z	LETTERS	FIGURES	SPACE	CHR. RETURN	LINE FEED
CODE 1	1	1		1	1	1				1	1						1		1		1		1	1	1	1	1	1			
2	2		2				2		2	2	2	2				2	2	2			2	2	2				2	2			2
CHART	o	o	o	o	o	o	o	o	o	o	o	o	o	o	o	o	o	o	o	o	o	o	o	o	o	o	o	o	o	o	o
3			3			3		3	3		3		3	3		3	3		3		3	3		3	3		3		3		
4		4	4	4		4	4			4	4		4	4	4			4				4		4			4	4		4	
5		5					5	5				5	5		5	5	5			5		5	5	5	5	5	5	5			

FIG. 47. *Top:* Five-channel tape. *Bottom:* Five-channel code.

Courtesy: Commercial Controls Corp., Rochester, N.Y.

FIG. 48. The Flexowriter Programatic prepares documents from unit edge-punched cards automatically. The machine reads, reproduces, or punches card or tape.

The edge-punched card is, as the name suggests, punched along the edge of the card. The code used is that of the five-channel perforated tape. Cards are easy to handle and file; however, the information on one card is limited by its length, generally about seven inches. This is sufficient, however, for many purposes. Figure 48 shows an office machine equipped to utilize edge-punched cards.

DISTINGUISHING FEATURES OF SDA

All SDA studies should first be systems-oriented and then machine-oriented. SDA demonstrates the need for using the systems approach in order to acquire the overall picture of what work is to be done where and how the total effort is coordinated toward achieving a given goal. This precedes the decisions pertaining to the mechanization of the data processing.

The preservation of source data, determined by thorough systems analysis to be necessary, in a mechanical and reusable form at the time of origination, is another distinguishing feature of SDA. All subsequent processing of the data is performed and preserved in this reusable form. The original data are (1) recorded at the point of origin in a mechanized form, (2) processed exclusively in a mechanized form, and (3) utilized in all subsequent operations, where needed, resulting in the integration of the processing work.

SDA is flexible. Machines can be added or subtracted, and the sequence of operations can be changed as requirements of data processing change. With its building block approach, SDA can be engineered to fit a variety of individual needs. Furthermore, nonrepetitive and special entries can be made manually without disrupting the normal progress of the work.

A detailed analysis of the work requirements and how they will be accomplished must be made. Every step of the system followed requires study to insure that the language prepared at one point is exactly as required at another point of use. The selection of the machines and the media also warrant careful analysis.

Although economic considerations are not always governing, quite frequently SDA must be justified on that basis. Usually some equipment is added to make the installation, redesign of office forms may be needed, and retraining of office personnel is required. A detailed cost and time analysis comparing the present to the proposed means of performing the work is essential.

ACHIEVING SDA

The applications of SDA are practically limitless. Every major system either by itself or along with other systems, offers possibilities. The gains to be realized are usually substantial. For best results, a definite program should be followed, patterned along these steps:

1. *Review areas and departments for study.* This can be started by preparing check lists revealing pertinent facts about present paper work activities in the manufacturing, procuring, and distributing departments. Information on the present methods of preparing papers, and their route or travel in the normal operation of the business, is the type to be obtained. By studying and evaluating this information, specific goals will emerge, such as improving production control communication, reducing processing time for purchase orders, providing quick shipping information, sending out invoices promptly, and eliminating copying errors.

2. *Secure top management approval.* Being integrated, SDA will cross departmental lines, involve many employees from different organizational units, and affect what they do. Hence, authorization of and support for the SDA effort must be given by top management; otherwise, the program will be seriously hampered, and little, if anything, will come of it.

3. *Appoint director to head all SDA activity.* With its blessing, top management should appoint an individual to manage the activity, giving him the necessary authority and help to direct the study to a successful installation. Designated groups, carefully selected, should be appointed to assist the director in finding and evaluating all the necessary facts. These groups will include members from the departments affected by proposed changes, systems and procedures personnel, and possibly specialists from a management consultant firm.

4. *Establish target dates.* SDA programs have a tendency to bog down or to extend over long periods unless they are controlled and adherence to a definite schedule is maintained. Target dates for completion of work should be established for each major element in the program. Activities such as finding the facts, charting and analyzing present systems and procedures, and determining recommendations seem to go on and on and unless specific dates for their completion are established and enforced.

5. *Gather and analyze pertinent information.* Many details are required, and suitable forms should be used for securing them in order to expedite identification, comparison, and evaluation. All participating members must be supplied proper instruction, so that they observe and understand what information to obtain and how to record it. The analysis should seek to disclose the major advantags and the disadvantages of the present manner of performing the work.

6. *Make recommendation and install.* As study and analysis proceed, possibilities for improvement are disclosed and verified. Substantiation of all gains should be made. Decisions must be made regarding what office

machines are to be used and what arrangement of the information on the paper forms will be followed. Finally, the proposal of what to do and why is presented to all interested management members, followed by a discussion to modify the proposal if necessary, but primarily to secure full agreement and approval. As soon as practical thereafter, the installation of the program should commence.

In applying the above steps, certain guides are helpful. These include the following: (1) Permit no restricted areas; instead, make the program comprehensive and truly integrated; (2) code first-hand material as much as possible in order to reduce future looking-up time; (3) use an adequate number of control totals between transmissions of data to insure accuracy; and (4) relate data from various sources and for various purposes to the greatest possible extent.

ILLUSTRATIONS OF SDA

Many applications of recording and accounting are handled simply and effectively by the use of a multientry, flexible-unit combination called Cardatype. The basic machine units include a typewriter, an auxiliary keyboard unit, and a card-feeding and -reading control console. These are illustrated in Figure 49.

Consider a manufacturer with a large number of customers. A punched card is prepared in advance for each customer, showing name and address.

Courtesy: International Business Machines Corp., New York

FIG. 49. Basic machine units for a Cardatype installation.

Also, a separate card is prepared for each item sold, providing information such as the item's description, weight, and price. These are kept in a reservoir file convenient to the operator. Upon receipt of a purchase order, the customer's name card and the cards for each of the items ordered are pulled from the file and fed into the feeding and reading control console, which actuates the typewriter, causing information on the cards to be typed on the paper forms. Semipermanent information, such as preliminary digits of a serial number or the date, is handled by means of the auxiliary keyboard unit, while variable or individualized information is manually typed on the paper forms by means of the typewriter. If it is desired, simultaneously with the writing of the forms, a punched card or a perforated tape can be produced for subsequent processing of the information in a different format for different purposes. Figure 50 shows examples of billing performed by this system. Note that the invoice, invoice register, stock selection tickets, and shipping tags are produced. Only the information encircled was inserted by manual key strokes; the rest, or over 95 percent of the work, is automatic—obtained by automating the source data. Several typewriters can be used, if necessary. The console unit performs all computations, such as tax, discount, and net amount. While the unit is handling one invoice, the operator refiles the cards from the previous invoice, so that they are ready for reuse as needed.

Figure 51 illustrates an interesting application of SDA for a national manufacturer having four widely separated plants. All production scheduling, stock control, receiving and billing of customers' orders, releases to manufacture, and routing of shipments are made from the centralized office located in a large city, different from that of any of the plants. All customers' orders sent direct to one of the plants by customers are immediately forwarded to the central office. Referring to Figure 51, and beginning at the left, the sequence is as follows. Customers' orders are received; edge-punched cards are pulled for customer name and for products ordered, and are sent to the Flexowriter with auxiliary tape perforator. Insertion of the edge-punched cards into the Flexowriter reader causes a six-part invoice and two perforated tapes of the transaction to be typed automatically. Tape No. 1 is sent to a Teletype machine, which, using the tape, transmits the order by means of electrical energy to the proper plant. The tape made at the receiving unit of the plant is used to write a five-part bill of lading and packing slip. Tape No. 2 from the Flexowriter is used in a tape-to-punched card converter. Two sets of punched cards are prepared, one set being used by general accounting accounts receivable, the other set being used for statistical analysis purposes and tabulated open orders file. Plant shipments are teletyped daily to the central office. Upon notice of shipment, the invoice copies are

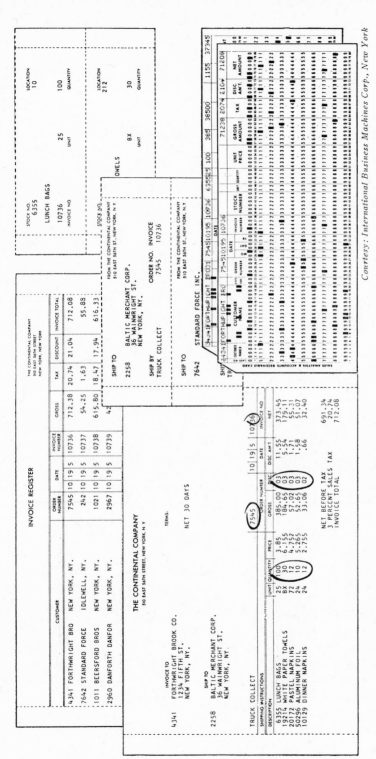

FIG. 50. Different papers pertaining to billing filled out simultaneously by Cardatype installation. Only the encircled portions were written by manually operating the typewriter.

Courtesy: International Business Machines Corp., New York

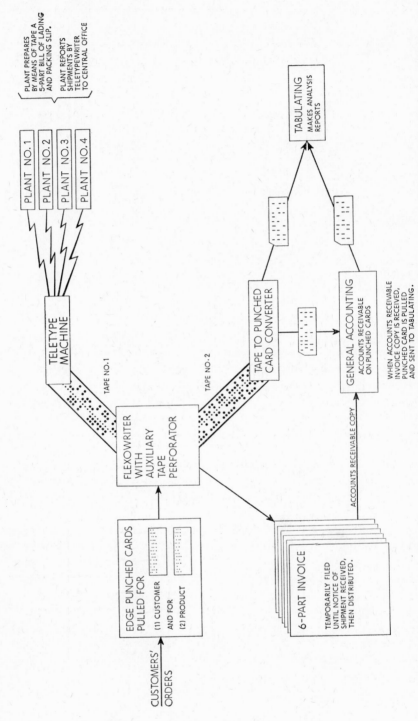

FIG. 51. Integrated data processing of order entry, shipping, and billing by a national manufacturer with a centralized office and four widely separated plants.

Labels within the figure:

PLANT PREPARES BY MEANS OF TAPE A 5-PART BILL OF LADING AND PACKING SLIP.

PLANT REPORTS SHIPMENTS BY TELETYPEWRITER TO CENTRAL OFFICE

PLANT NO. 1
PLANT NO. 2
PLANT NO. 3
PLANT NO. 4

TELETYPE MACHINE

TAPE NO. 1

FLEXOWRITER WITH AUXILIARY TAPE PERFORATOR

TAPE NO. 2

TAPE TO PUNCHED CARD CONVERTER

TABULATING
MAKES ANALYSIS REPORTS

GENERAL ACCOUNTING
ACCOUNTS RECEIVABLE ON PUNCHED CARDS

WHEN ACCOUNTS RECEIVABLE INVOICE COPY IS RECEIVED, PUNCHED CARD IS PULLED AND SENT TO TABULATING.

ACCOUNTS RECEIVABLE COPY

EDGE PUNCHED CARDS PULLED FOR
(1) CUSTOMER
AND FOR
(2) PRODUCT

CUSTOMERS' ORDERS

6-PART INVOICE
TEMPORARILY FILED UNTIL NOTICE OF SHIPMENT RECEIVED, THEN DISTRIBUTED.

distributed, the accounts receivable copy being sent to general accounting, upon receipt of which the punched card of the transaction in their possession is pulled and sent to tabulating, where costs and other reports are prepared.

As indicated in this example, a Teletype machine can be used to transmit the taped information to the various plants. Improvements in communication equipment have been so rapid, however, that it is now possible to send economically and conveniently huge quantities of data over the telephone wires. This is discussed later in this chapter under Data-Phone. Further, machines are available that expedite and combine data collection, handling, and transmission. Specifically, fixed and semi-fixed data (customer's name, address, terms, etc.) are obtained from a perforated tape, variable data (date, quantity, etc.) from the machine's keyboard, thus supplying a finished paper product with carbons for processing and filing. In addition, a perforated composite tape of the complete document is made and can be transmitted simultaneously by the machine to several destinations at the same time (cross-country or cross-office), or to a computer, or placed in storage. Figure 52 shows the machine offering these advantages.

Mention should also be made of "turn-around documents." Public utility bills on punched cards, magnetic ink bank checks, and bank loan payment forms are representative of turn-around documents now in use.[1] These papers are machine produced, sent to customers, and returned for further processing—typical of SDA. The initial data do not have to be rewritten in order to perform the additional processing. Also, it is possible for the customer to tabulate or process the data in a number of ways for his own purposes prior to returning the document. This practice is common when the customer is a company or a bank. The use of turn-around documents normally results in faster response in returning documents because they can be processed immediately upon receipt and without costly preparation for processing.

A rapidly expanding application is Numerical Control (NC). Some prefer to call it symbolic control. Logically, it can be considered a part of the general area of SDA. NC is an automatic means of operating a factory machine by feeding a previously prepared punched tape or card with all instructions in numerical form into a mechanism that directs the machine. A computer can also be used, but it is not essential in many NC applications. Computers are more likely to be employed for controlling complete processes such as metal-rolling mills and chemical production than for discrete parts manufacturing.[2] NC instructions are detailed and

---

[1] See also Chapter 7, pp. 147–50.

[2] See Chapter 9, pp. 184–85.

FIG. 52. An automated communications set receives, integrates, transmits, and disseminates messages and data of all kinds. The unit illustrated features dual readers that automatically interoperate, a tape punch that simultaneously prints and perforates, and a four-row alphanumeric typewriter keyboard. Its operating speed is 10 characters per second or the equivalent of 100 words per minute.

include every step required to operate the machine in order to obtain a machined part exactly according to blueprint specifications. The old concept of the operator's "running" the machine is eliminated. Basically there are two fundamental types of numerical controlling: (1) positioning and (2) contouring. The former deals with getting the tool and the material in the desired relationship, after which the tool is advanced either automatically or manually to perform the required work. The second type, or contouring, requires that the path of the tool be controlled continuously. In fact, this type is commonly referred to as the "continuous-path" method. There is constant synchronization of the movement of the tool in several axes. Among the advantages of NC are (1) more machine utilization time, less machine setup time, and lower lead times; (2) elimination of fixtures and templates used as guides in manual means; (3) less inspection and fewer rejects; and (4) feasibility of machining otherwise "impossible" parts.

NC has wide application in metalworking, including use with machines for drilling, milling, planning, routing, welding, riveting, tube bending, and

Courtesy: Giddings & Lewis Machine Tool Co., Fond du Lac, Wis.

FIG. 53. A vertical-spindle machine equiped with Giddings and Lewis Numeridrill featuring five-second automatic tool changer and program combinations of spindle motions for drilling, tapping, boring, milling, and jump feeds. A three-axis control is standard equipment but special controls can be furnished.

coil winding. Figure 53 shows a vertical-spindle machine equipped with a Giddings and Lewis Numeridrill (numerical control), made up as shown in the figure of the pedestal-mounted control unit which is immediately back of the operator, and the cabinet housing the electrical control circuits which is located to the operator's right and to the rear of the illustration. This vertical-spindle machine with Numeridrill features an automatic tool changer, removing one tool from the spindle and replacing it with another within a time of five seconds.

Large department stores have the problem of inventory control so that the proper quantity and quality of each item are on hand in order to maximize sales and gross margins. To help solve this problem economically, SDA is being used. At the time a customer transaction is originally entered into a National Cash Register, a perforated tape recording is made. The recording shows cash or credit sale; salesperson's number; customer's number; description of merchandise, including material, size, style, and retail price; and the vendor's number. A prepunched price ticket—actually a small card about 2½ inches wide and 1 inch long—inserted in a unit called a Media Reader automatically starts the tape recorder and produces a detailed record of the item sold. Complete information on inventory control, by units, is thus accurately and economically provided. Figure 54 illustrates the machine, tape, and price ticket used for this purpose.

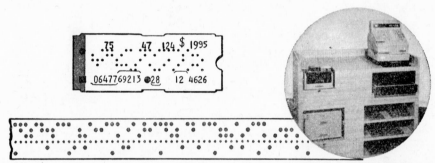

Courtesy: National Cash Register Co., Dayton

FIG. 54. Machine, perforated tape, and price ticket used for effective unit inventory control by large retail outlets.

SDA AND THE COMPUTER

SDA sometimes includes the use of a computer. This is the case when widely dispersed common office machines are connected with a computer in a central location. When any of the dispersed machines mechanizes the source data which are utilized by the computer serving as the central processing unit, or vice versa, the element of joining machines together for integrating the data processing can be viewed as SDA and a computer. To illustrate, consider a centralized accounting operation that requires that information be consolidated from source data received from widespread locations. This arrangement is shown by Figure 55. Data can be sent to the computer headquarters by mail, messenger service, telegraph, or telephone. For any of these communication means, the data can be sent in computer language, but telegraph or telephone provides much faster

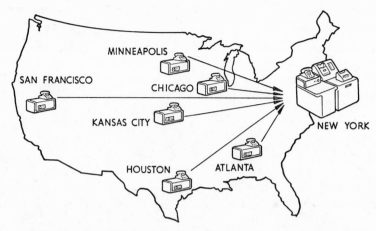

FIG. 55. Centralized accounting arangement requiring data from widespread locations.

service. Telegraph has been used extensively, but developments now tie the ordinary telephone to a computer and provide multiple and direct access to it. The development making this possible is called Data-Phone; the machine utilized is illustrated by Figure 56.

Regular telephone lines comprising a nationwide network are used, and there are no intermediate steps. To utilize the Data-Phone, a customer picks up the telephone and dials the service number. A dial tone signals connection, after which he inserts an identification card into the device attached to the telephone, which identification is required by the computer and confirms the customer's right to order. Then, the data, in the language of the computer—punched cards, perforated tape, or magnetic tape—are fed into the device; and these data are transmitted at speeds of up to 1,600 words a minute directly into the computer.[3] Machines talk to one another, cross-town or cross-country. Payment for each Data-Phone call is made just like an ordinary telephone call. Its potential is believed to be so great that in the not too distant future, conversations between machines over regular telephone lines may exceed the volume of voice communications.

ADVANTAGES OF SDA

Why the widespread adoption of SDA? Some of the more obvious reasons are implied in the above discussion, but several additional comments are warranted. By employing machines adapted to use common

---

[3] Magnetic tape for computers is discussed in Chapter 7, p. 144.

Courtesy: Illinois Bell Telephone Co., Chicago

FIG. 56.   The units to the left constitute Data-Phone. To the right, punched cards are being prepared.

language media, much repetitive data processing can be accomplished with a minimum of manual effort. SDA is especially effective where a large part of the data is constant and is continually reproduced from day to day and from paper to paper. There are many such applications in the typical enterprise. In addition, SDA provides practically error-proof processing. Once the data are correctly put into the medium subsequent errors in processing are normally nonexistent. In contrast, with ordinary manual recording and processing of the same data, errors are committed at various points and seem to defy efforts to eliminate them. SDA also lends itself to handling large volumes of data. The machine operations are fast and constant, and machine downtime is held to a minimum. A volume almost impossible to handle within a given period by manual means can be processed efficiently by SDA. Furthermore, deadlines can be met. The processed data are kept current and can be used while they are fresh and in keeping with present requirements.

CHAPTER SEVEN

COMPUTERS—TECHNICAL

CONSIDERATIONS

How can great minds be produced in a country where the
test of great minds is agreeing with the opinions of small minds?
—John Stuart Mill

THE LAST of the three major considerations of the office technology is computers. We will first discuss the main technical considerations of this area, thus gaining a background for a better understanding of the managerial considerations and interesting applications of computers which are set forth in the following two chapters.

A computer is actually a group of mechanical and electronic devices connected into a unit or system to process data. Accurately designated, a computer is an electronic data-processing system. Here is a unit that can take a bundle of facts, process the necessary string of operations, including any or all eight of the basic elements of data processing discussed in Chapter 4, turn out the answers with fabulous rapidity and without error, and proceed automatically to the next bundle of data and process them.

BASIC TYPES OF COMPUTERS

The basic types of computers are (1) digital, (2) analog, and (3) hybrid digital-analog. Digital computers, or arithmetic machines as they are sometimes described, deal with actual numbers and their answer is a set of numbers or letters, which can be made as accurate as desired. These computers perform according to a set of instructions, or a program, and if required, will perform hundreds and hundreds of repetitive calculations. A digital computer performs the work immediately after it is given a problem. It is a common type of machine for processing business data and represents by far the greatest number of computers in operation today.

An analog computer operates on the basis of using a formula or system to represent that which is being investigated or by duplicating mathematical behavior. It can instantaneously solve a mathematical equation with ten variables. It is actually based on approximations, and both input and output of an analog computer are approximate positions on a continuous scale rather than absolute numbers. Results from the analog computer are never precisely accurate, but they are commonly within 1/20 of 1 percent, which is entirely satisfactory for most applications. Calculating flows and pressures in pipelines and the position of a moving target are accomplished by an analog computer in only a split second, whereas for the same application the digital computer would calculate enormous quantities of data for an hour or so. Many analog computers are used for research and scientific investigation.

A hybrid digital-analog computer is a combination of the first two, digital and analog, utilized to obtain a computer capable of more work than the two can accomplish working separately. This hybrid type is a more recent development. It has been used advantageously for outer space projects and satellite programs. To date there are relatively few hybrid digital-analog computers in use.

THREE TECHNICAL CONSIDERATIONS

To simplify this duscussion of technical considerations, we can organize our thoughts around three fundamental subject areas. These are: (1) the anatomy of a computer, (2) programming work for computer processing, and (3) coding work for computer processing. The first deals with the essential makeup of a computer. The term, *hardware,* is used to identify the computer itself and its various accessories. The second includes preparing the work for computer handling. The third, or coding, deals with putting the work in a form or language that the computer can handle *Software* is commonly used to identify all programming and coding required to utilize the computer, i.e., to utilize the *hardware* effectively.

THE ANATOMY OF A COMPUTER

The top portion of Figure 57 diagrams the essential makeup of an electronic computer; the bottom portion, the general appearance of actual units. Different models will vary somewhat in detail and specific purposes, but the fundamentals outlined here are common to all computers.

Data in a suitable form such as punched cards, perforated paper tape,

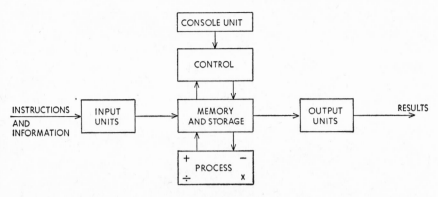

Courtesy: International Business Machines Corp., New York

FIG. 57. Basic components of an electronic computer.

or magnetic tape are fed into the input units, where the data are converted into so-called computer language or, more accurately, electric pulses. These data are stored or retained in a memory unit of the computer. The memory units hold standard or current facts and sometimes instructions. When needed, the data are released to the process or computer section.

Directing the entire operation is the control section, which issues a program, or chain of instructions, to the process unit for each new group of data. It can send stored data required by the program, examine any step to select the following one, and start the processing of the next group of data. Frequently, a console unit, illustrated by Figure 58, permits a human operator to enter data if necessary, determine the status of the

FIG. 58.   Computer system console unit.

operations, and exercise complete supervision of the processing work. By means of the output units, completed processed data are printed and made available for use.

BASIC OPERATIONAL UNITS

From what has been stated it follows that a series of planned operations are applied to data for processing. These data are entered into the computer by means of an input unit and processed according to pro-grammed instructions by utilizing this input or data already stored within the computer. The end result of the processing is obtained from the computer by means of the output unit. This means that a computer has (1) input-output units, (2) memory and storage units, (3) processing units, and (4) a console controlling unit.

INPUT-OUTPUT UNITS

Input units supply data to the computer. They "read" data from punched cards, perforated tape, magnetic tape, or magnetic ink characters and make them available to memory and storage units of the computer. Output units convert the processed data from the computer by transfer-ring the "computer language" to a suitable form, such as printed records, punched cards, perforated paper tape, or magnetic tape. In the processing of business data very large quantities of input and of output must be handled. Some output units have a speed equivalent to printing the amount of print on one page of this book in about two seconds. Expressed differently, this is the equivalent of 7,500 paychecks printed in less than one hour.

However, the operating speeds of input-output units are commonly lower than those of the computer processing unit and hence limit the total operation. To alleviate this condition, the computer is used to perform other internal operations on available data while the input data are being fed in, or other devices are employed to perform relatively simple handling and transcribing work. A buffer type of device is also utilized to minimize interruption to the computer processing unit. A buffer is actually an auxiliary storage device which receives data at high speed from the

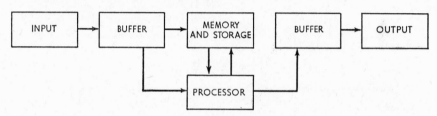

FIG. 59.   Illustrating the use of buffering in computer operation.

processor, returns control to the processor, and then either feeds the data at high speeds to the processor, or accepts data at high speeds from the processor. This is shown in Figure 59.

The term *throughput* and its efficiency are used to explain this same idea of acquiring a maximum of data flow, not in, or not out of the computer, but through the computer. In most data processing it is throughput that governs the performance. That is, the quantity of data taken in, processed, and put out as completed results should be maximized for best computer operation.

MEMORY AND STORAGE DEVICES

These devices make up the components of the computer capable of storing information which is subject to recall or reference. Varying in type, size, and capacity, the memory and storage devices also serve to store programmed instructions and to provide work area for editing. All data to be processed must pass through what is commonly referred to as "main storage." This storage is supplemented by secondary storage units, which are not directly accessible to the processing unit but instead are connected to the processing unit through the main storage.

Each register, or location, in a memory unit holds one *word*. This may consist of up to 20 digits or letters. A "word" is the basic measurement of storage capacity. Typically, a computer will have 10,000–15,000 registers, but some large scale machines contain up to 300,000 registers. Since references are made to memory and storage units during the processing, the accessibility and capacity of these units and their operation in the computer are paramount. Specifically, we are concerned about the time required to refer to a specific register (location) and obtain the information from it. This is known as *access time*. In addition, the storage capacity of the memory and storage unit is important for we must have enough registers to handle all the information to be processed.

Memory and storage devices in use today are:

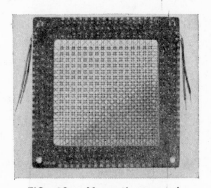

FIG. 60.   Magnetic core plane as used in a computer.

1. *Magnetic core.* This is illustrated in Figure 60. It consists of a series of very tiny cores, or rings of magnetizable material, with wire passed through the opening in two directions. When an electric current is sent through the wires in one direction the core becomes magnetized with a positive charge; in contrast, when the current is sent through the wire in the opposite direction the core becomes magnetized with a negative charge. Thus, the core stores either a positive or negative value, an on or off condition, which represents a portion of a binary configuration.[1]

Magnetic core offers compact size and relatively low access time. The number of cores in a plane and the number of planes determine the storage capacity. Advances in computer design seem to indicate that, for the magnetic core, future reduction in the cost per storage location is a distinct possibility. Access time now is in excess of 4,000 registers per second, which is well above that for any other storage medium.

2. *Magnetic drum.* A magnetically coated surface of a cylindrically shaped object is the data-bearing medium of a magnetic drum. The data are coded in the form of the location of magnetic spots or dots on this

---

[1] See page 139 for discussion of binary configuration.

surface.[2] Figure 61 illustrates the magnetic drum means. A magnetic drum is mounted on its axis and is rotated to bring the desired information to a magnetic head that reads the information. More than 1,000 characters can be stored within a square inch of surface and are available at a rate of about 25,000 characters per second.

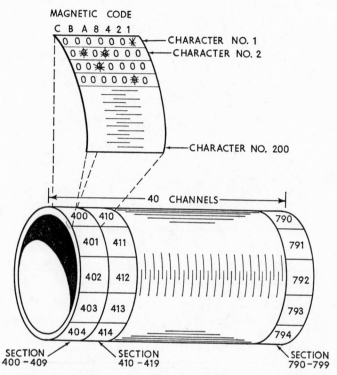

FIG. 61. Magnetic drum storage. In this illustration there are 200 characters per section, 10 sections per channel, and 40 channels per drum. This makes 80,000 characters per drum.

3. *Magnetic disk*. This medium is similar to a phonograph record. The disks are about two feet in diameter, coated on both sides with ferrous oxide recording material, and mounted on a vertical shaft. Data are coded and stored as magnetized spots located in concentric tracks. Reading heads mounted on access arms read or write as directed by the computer controlling unit. Storage efficiency is satisfactory, access time is accepta-

---

[2] See also coding of information under magnetic tape, pp. 144–45.

ble and if need be can be reduced by using several access arms and "read-write" heads.

4. *Magnetic tape.* This medium can be described as a metallic or plastic ribbon of tape with a magnetic surface. Data for storage is coded and recorded on the tape as spots similar to that of the magnetic drum or disk. Magnetic tape is a common medium for secondary storage. It has too great an access time for wide usage as the medium for main storage. Magnetic tape is widely used for handling input and output data, as discussed later in this chapter.

PROCESSING UNITS

There is always a central processing unit made up of a control and arithmetic-logical section. The former integrates automatically the operation of the entire computer system in keeping with the program of instructions. This includes controlling the data within the computer such as regulating the input devices, moving data into or out of memory and storage units, and between memory and storage units and the arithmetic-logical section, and controlling data entering the output units.

As its name implies, the arithmetic-logical section performs arithmetic and logical operations. These include performing according to algebraic equations and calculus as well as basic processing operations such as reading, sorting, transmitting, comparing, and storing.

CONSOLE CONTROLLING UNIT

By means of this unit the operator can gain a continual picture of the internal operations of the computer. One can view the console controlling unit as actually an integral part of the central processing unit. The operator can start and stop the computer, interrogate for data in memory units, and load data into the computer by means of the console controlling unit. With reference to programming, it is possible to use sense switches to stop processing or to select predetermined program paths. Hence, the flexibility of the program is increased.

There are also cases where not all the program is stored in and accessible to the computer. In such cases, by means of the console controlling unit, programs can be entered directly into the computer step by step as the processing work progresses. Also, the console controlling unit permits tracing a system or a procedure one step at a time and affords high human operator or external control. In some instances, limited data can be entered directly by control buttons on the console. In addition, limited output information may be obtained, thus enabling the console operator to supervise the computer operation.

GLOSSARY OF COMPUTER TERMS

At this point it will be helpful to insert Figure 62. This glossary of selected terms used with computers serves as a convenient review and reference for computer terminology. Familiarity with these terms will assist in grasping the technical significance of computer operation. Some of the terms included in this list concern programming and coding, which will now be discussed.

Accumulator—a storage register where results are accumulated.

Alphameric Characters—letters of the alphabet, numerical digits, or symbols used for communicative purposes.

Analog Computer—one representing variables by physical analogies in continuous form. An analog computer is said to measure, not count.

Batch Processing—the means by which a number of similar input items are grouped for processing during the same machine run.

Buffer Storage—the temporary storing of information during a transfer of that information. Buffer storage is used to permit simultaneous computation and input or output.

Checkout—the determination of the correctness of the computer routine, locating errors in it, and correcting them.

Compile—to produce a machine-language routine by translating from ordinary or non-machine program. Concerns programming.

Digital Computer—a computer in which information is processed and represented in discrete form. A digital computer counts; it does not measure.

Hardware—the mechanical and electrical devices making up a computer.

Library—an organized collection of proven and standard routines which can be incorporated into larger routines.

Location—a place in a storage unit where a unit of data or an instruction may be stored.

Loop—a technique of coding in programming whereby a group of instructions is repeated with alterations of some of the instructions and usually with modification of the data being processed.

Off-Line—the operation of input or output devices are not under direct control of the central processing unit.

On-Line—the operation of input or output devices are under direct control of the central processing unit.

Parameter—a quantity to which arbitrary values may be assigned for such things as decimal point location, record format, and size.

Parity Check—a checking means based on making a total number of "on" or "off" in some grouping of binary digits.

Random Access—the finding and getting of data in storage is relatively independent of the location of the information most recently obtained.

Real Time Computation—data processing by which the computer supplies information to a business activity whenever the information is demanded.

Register—a device that holds information while or until it is used.

Software—the programming and coding work required for effective computer data processing.

FIG. 62. Glossary of common terms used in computer technology.

PROGRAMMING

The designing of a computer program was discussed in Chapter 2. However, for purposes of emphasis as well as convenience to the immediate discussion, certain basic facts will be reiterated. A data-processing system is designed to handle a specific number and type of operations. When included in the system, a computer is directed to perform each basic element of processing by specific instructions, which normally include the identification of the data, the basic elements to be performed, the sequence, and what to do with the results. This complete package of instructions is commonly known as a program. It is developed by "programming," which can be considered as the breaking-down in most complete detail of the work to be electronically processed.

For example, assume that the processing requires multiplication. In this case, the computer must be informed or directed to perform multiplication as well as (1) the operation that precedes the multiplying, (2) the operation that follows the multiplying, (3) the identity and location of the multiplicand, and (4) likewise that of the multiplier. In addition, after the multiplication is completed, the result must be transferred to storage at a specific location in the storage device, from whence it can be discharged, if desired, by the output device or retained in storage for future processing, as the individual case might be. There are certain exceptions to this, however, as for example when magnetic tape ledger records are used as the input medium, in which case part of the stored data are on the tape or strips of the ledgers. Also, in the case of magnetic ink characters being used as the input medium, little of the data is stored in a storage unit of the computer.[3]

In other words, an operation usually involves a chain of operations such as reading, locating information in storage, transferring to the processing device, processing, returning the result to storage, perhaps also returning the initial information to storage, sending out the result from storage to the output device, and finally discharging the result in the prescribed medium from the output device. Thus, the simplest portion of a procedure requires a number of carefully planned steps that must be designated in extreme detail to the computer.

Hence, by means of computer programming, the machine progresses by moving from one minute element of work to the next in a prescribed sequence. In some instances, the sequential element can be either of two possibilities but no more, represented by yes or no, go or no go, on or off,

---

[3] Magnetic tape ledger records and magnetic ink characters are discussed later in this chapter, pp. 145–48.

and so forth. If the answer is "Yes," for example, the computer follows the element of this designation. In contrast, if the answer is "No," the alternate element is followed. This means that minute, detailed, sequential steps in the work to be done must be set forth, and where choices arise, the decision must be one of the two alternatives. The computer having the information of the precise element can determine if "yes" or "no" is to be followed. This is illustrated humorously but helpfully by Figure 63.

Since a computer program is usually designed and evolved in the form of a flow chart listing the precise step-by-step action to be taken, it is extremely helpful in performing programming work to have an intimate knowledge of existing systems, procedures, and methods. The broad, overall picture should be taken, for one large programming job may encompass many small jobs, thus eliminating duplication and needless waste. In addition, a complete understanding of the purpose for which the finished data are used appears paramount in this work. To illustrate the breadth and detail of this work, it is common for the preparation of customers' invoices to require 1,500 or more steps.

When instructions in the form of programs are placed in the storage device of a computer, they are commonly termed *stored programs*. One computer can be supplied with a number of different programs for different work by simply putting in, or loading, the programs into storage. The stored programs are accessible to the computer, providing it with the ability to alter its own program in response to conditions revealed as the processing takes place. Hence, it can be said that the computer exercises some judgment within the limits established by the programmed operations to be performed. In this sense, it can be stated that computers are capable of making simple decisions.

BUSINESS AND DATA-PROCESSING PROGRAMMING

Progress in programming has been significant to those wishing to use computers for the processing of normal business data. Typically, this type of work requires many programs providing for relatively small amounts of processing to large quantities of data. Comparatively simple additions, multiplications, and recordings are required. Programming is especially important in adopting computers for business purposes.

In contrast, the use of the computer for research and much scientific work entails a small amount of data being processed many, many times. Frequently, the task of processing is to substitute various values in mathematical formulas and determine whether a critical value, such as the stress in a structure or the amount of chemical produced, is within a safe, allowable technical limit. Processing data for scientific work frequently

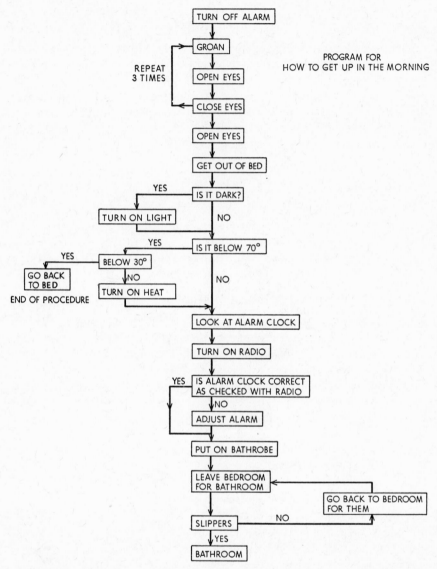

FIG. 63. This diagram illustrates how programmers have to instruct the electronic system to work.

involves complex mathematics such as extracting square roots, raising numbers to decimal powers as exponents, and handling repetitive processing using different numerical values. Programming for the computer, especially the analog type, to handle this type of work is fairly simple.

It is interesting to note that computers were first used for scientific work, insofar as large-scale commercial usage is concerned. This was probably due to the restricting influence of programming in connection with the computer use. We simply had not figured out how to tell the computer economically the manner of handling much data with little processing. However, during the past decade or so, the rapid strides in the advancement of programming and the knowledge being built up about it are probably the most outstanding factors contributing to computer progress for the processing of ordinary business data.

COMMON BUSINESS ORIENTED LANGUAGE (COBOL)

To operate a computer, it is necessary to have a network of preprogrammed packages which range from simple service routines to highly complex compilers. A compiler accepts a special code or a natural language, interprets it for the computer, selects the proper routine from a library retained by the computer, supervises the coding, allocates data, assembles a complete program, and gives a report on this program. The first compilers were all algebraic or mathematical, because the language of mathematics is concise and definite. With time, however, attempts were made to orientate the input language of a compiler to the natural language of the user. Subsequently "Math-Matic," "Fortran," and "Unicode" were developed.

With the great interest developing in computers for processing business data, efforts were directed and stimulated toward developing new system languages more suitable for this type of processing. As a result, "Flow-Matic" was pioneered, followed shortly by "AIMACO" and "FACT." The situation seemed to be that each computer manufacturer was developing his own language, a condition not only costly and unnecessary, but extremely difficult for users of several different types of computers. Accordingly, in January, 1960, the Conference on Data Systems Languages, or CODASYL, accepted and approved a plan for perfecting and advancing a common and simplified English language for business system programming. This simplified language is called COBOL and stands for Common Business Oriented Language. Figure 64 illustrates COBOL.

This advance toward a common computer language suitable for all computers, regardless of their manufacture, is the most significant advance in programming. Once a program is written in COBOL, it need not be rewritten if switching from one data-processing system to another takes place. Exchange of business programs is therefore expedited. Costly and time-consuming rewriting from one machine language to another is eliminated, and the burden of programming is eased by the use of

This language is COBOL:

SUBTRACT QUANTITY-SOLD FROM BALANCE-ON-HAND. IF BALANCE-ON-HAND IS NOT LESS THAN REORDER-LEVEL THEN GO TO BALANCE-OK ELSE COMPUTE QUANTITY-TO-BUY. . . .

COBOL eliminates the use of detailed and difficult computer language instructions such as:

06011	'	12040	12047
06028	C	12048	
06074	?	12046	12014
06145	S	12012	12010

FIG. 64.   COBOL permits instructions to computers with simple English words of everyday business language.

COBOL. As an indirect result of the COBOL influence, many business-oriented "canned" or subroutine programs have been created for each type of computer. Also, automatic compilers and translators have appeared on the market. Thus, another hurdle has been removed, so that the progress of computer processing of business data can continue upward to even greater heights.

CODING THE WORK FOR COMPUTER PROCESSING

The third and last fundamental subject area in technical considerations of computers is coding the work for computer processing. All information is conveyed by symbols. In the English language, there are familiar letters of the alphabet, numbers, and punctuation marks. For everyday correspondence, these symbols are recorded on paper according to a prescribed sequence and grouping. When transported to another person reading and writing English, these symbols convey a particular message.

In the same manner, to communicate with a computer system necessitates that the information be expressed in symbols and in a form that can be read and interpreted by data-processing devices. In the case of the computer, this language has been called "computerese." It is language the machine can understand and act upon, in keeping with the desired processing. Man invented "computerese" to utilize the machines. It represents symbols making up a mutual language to provide communication between people and machines. In other words, every detail which the machine is to follow must be put into language that the machine can handle. This includes the use of special codes and numbers which, put on or into the data-transmitting medium, will cause the machine to perform the operation desired.

There are a number of different media that can be used. For input data, the following are included: (1) punched card, (2) perforated paper tape, (3) magnetic tape, (4) magnetic tape ledger record, (5) magnetic ink characters, and (6) imprints of specially formed characters or fonts that are read by machine. The processing of output data, being basically the reverse of that for input data, means that the same media can be used for output data as for input data. However, since output data are either for human use or for subsequent machine use of a relatively limited sort, not all the communication input media are used for output. For the latter purpose, the communication media include (1) punched card (2) perforated paper tape, (3) magnetic tape, (4) magnetic tape ledger record, and (5) ordinary print on paper. The concept of input data, output data, and data processing by a computer is shown by Figure 65.

BINARY MODE

Before discussing each of the data-transmitting media, some fundamentals in their representation of the data should be pointed out. The processing and storage of data within the computer are made possible by coding the data. The more common mode of coding is known as a binary mode, which involves the use of only two possible conditions. For example, holes in a paper tape are either present or absent. Likewise, magnetic spots are either present or absent, electric current is in one direction or in an opposite direction, switches are closed or open, and electric current is on or off. In other words, the base is two, just as decimals refer to a base of ten. Tubes, or transistors, or cores, can exist in only two states—"off" or "on," emitting or not, magnetized in one or the other charge.

One binary digit is called a *bit*. The common arrangement is the binary coded decimal whereby four bit positions represent from left to right the decimal digits, 8, 4, 2, 1. That is, different values are placed on the four positions and the sum of these positions for recording information. There is a combination of these four bit positions to represent any digit from 0 to 9. Figure 66 illustrates these combinations.

The handling of zero in a computer is usually noted as ten, i.e., an eight and a two. In the binary position this avoids registering all blanks for zero, for if we did this it would be difficult to determine whether the register is supposed to be zero or the machine has failed to transfer data. Other codes than binary are used by some computers including a numerical coding to the base eight, known as octal notation, a seven-bit

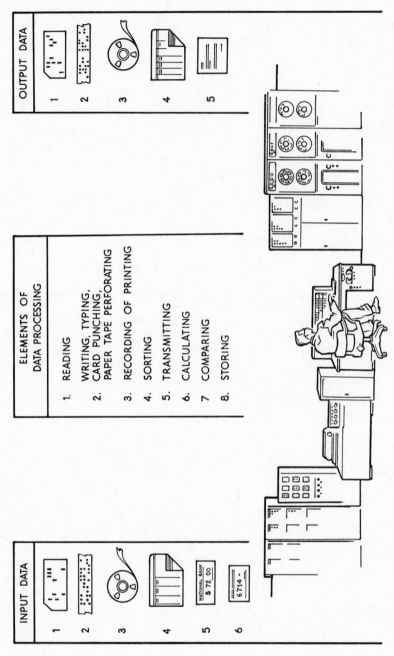

FIG. 65. Media of input data, processing, and media of output data of an electronic data-processing system.

INPUT DATA

1
2
3
4
5   NATIONAL BANK $ 72 00
6   6714 -

ELEMENTS OF DATA PROCESSING

1. READING
2. WRITING, TYPING, CARD PUNCHING, PAPER TAPE PERFORATING
3. RECORDING OF PRINTING
4. SORTING
5. TRANSMITTING
6. CALCULATING
7. COMPARING
8. STORING

OUTPUT DATA

1
2
3
4
5

BINARY CODE

DECIMAL	8	4	2	1	TOTAL VALUE (READ ACROSS)
	IS	REPRESENTED		BY	
0	0	0	0	0	0
1	0	0	0	✳	1
2	0	0	✳	0	2
3	0	0	✳	✳	3
4	0	✳	0	0	4
5	0	✳	0	✳	5
6	0	✳	✳	0	6
7	0	✳	✳	✳	7
8	✳	0	0	0	8
9	✳	0	0	✳	9

FIG. 66.   Illustrating the four bit position and values to represent decimal numbers. For decimal 5, the "bits" of "4" and "1" are "on," "8" and "2" are "off."

alphameric, a six-bit numerical, and a biquinary system indicating numbers to the base five. The number system followed is a technical consideration, and assistance in its understanding is offered by the computer manufacturer both before and after machine installation.

PUNCHED CARD

The typical punched card is about $7\frac{3}{8}$ inches long by $3\frac{1}{4}$ inches high. In the IBM type, the card is divided into 80 vertical columns, each one containing 12 units which, read from the top down, are: 12, 11, 0, 1, 2, 3, 4, 5, 6, 7, 8, 9. The 12 and the 11 zones are frequently called R and X, respectively. Data from original records are put on the cards by means of punched holes; that is, when certain holes are punched in the card, these holes represent definite information. High-speed machines are used for this purpose. The letters of the alphabet number 26, and there are 10 digits (0–9), making a total of 36 characters, each of which must be assigned to coded representation by a positioned hole in the card. Since there are 12 units in a vertical column on the card, it requires three different vertical arrangements totaling 36 (3 × 12) characters to represent all possibilities. This is clearly illustrated by Figure 67.

Information represented or coded by means of the presence or absence of holes in specific and exact locations is read as the card travels through a card-reading mechanism. The reading is automatically converted to an electronic language utilized by the computer in its data processing.

It is also possible to record binary information by the use of row

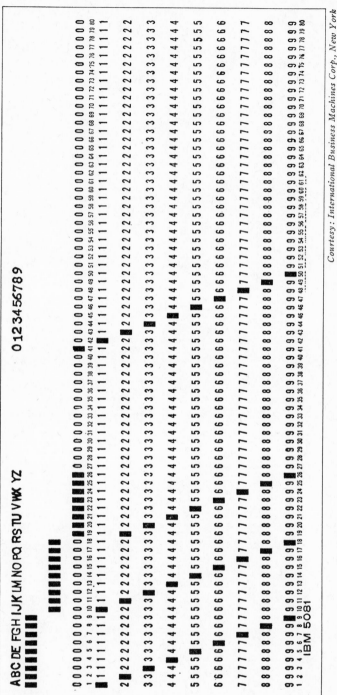

FIG. 67. A code used for punched holes which represent letter and figure data.

binary, in which the data are arranged serially across each row beginning at the lower left, moving across from left to right for each horizontal row, and progressively upward on the card. A punched hole in the card represents "yes," no punch indicates "no." It is also possible to arrange the binary information in parallel columns, with each column of the card containing 12 information bits. For certain computers, where the basic unit of information is a word consisting of a maximum of 36 consecutive bits, a total of three adjacent card columns is used.

PERFORATED PAPER TAPE

Another common medium for the transmission of data into a computer system is perforated paper tape. It is a continuous recording medium and can be used to record long runs of data, being limited only by the capacity of the storage medium into which the data are being placed.

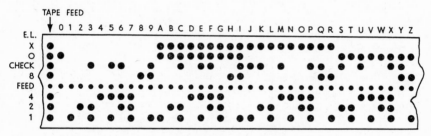

FIG. 68. Code for eight-channel perforated paper tape.

Most perforated paper tape is either of an eight-channel code or of a five-channel code. A channel runs the length of the tape. In any column across the width of the tape, the number of possible punching positions is equivalent to the number of channels of the tape. That is, in the eight-channel tape, there are eight possible punching positions; and in the five-channel tape, there are five positions.

Figure 68 shows the code of an eight-channel paper tape. Observe that the lower five channels, identified as channels 1, 2, 4, and 8, and "check," are used to record numerical characters. As already stated, the sum of the position values indicates the value of the character. For example, 3 is expressed by holes in positions 1, 2, and "check," while 7 consists of holes in 1, 2, and 4. For alphabetic characters, two additional channels at the top, X and O, are used with the 1, 2, 4, 8, and "check" channels. The arrangement is similar to that of the 12, 11, or R and X zones of the punched card being used in conjunction with the 0–9 or digit punches of the punched card. To illustrate, the letter A is represented by holes in the following channels: *X, O,* and 1; *K* by holes in channels *X,* "check," and 2.

The channel identified as "check" is used for verification purposes. Each column is punched with an odd number of holes. If the sum of the holes punched in channels *X, O,* 8, 4, 2, and 1 is an even number, a hole in the "check" channel must be present. This explains why the column for the letter *Y* shows holes in channels *O,* "check," and 8. The "end of line" or "El" channel at the top of the tape is used to indicate the end of a record or the tape.

MAGNETIC TAPE

The principal input medium for computer systems is magnetic tape. It is one-half inch wide, made of plastic, and coated on one side with a metallic oxide. Information recorded on magnetic tape is permanent, but

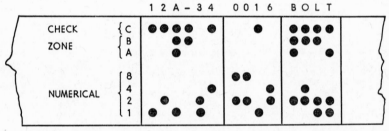

FIG. 69.   Coding of magnetic spots on tape to transmit information. This is the seven-bit alphameric code. Translation of the spots is shown at top of sketch.

previous recordings are destroyed as new information is put on the tape. It is possible to utilize the same tape many times, thus saving in recording costs. Magnetic tape is supplied on plastic reels containing approximately 2,400 feet of tape.

The data are recorded on the tape in the form of magnetic dots or spots. The code employed is illustrated by Figure 69. Starting at the top, the first channel is *C,* for checking, followed in order by *B* and *A,* commonly called zone tracks, and 8, 4, 2, and 1, the numerical tracks or channels. In similar manner to that described under binary mode and perforated tape, numbers are coded, using the numerical channels. The number 5 is coded as 4 and 1; and 7 is 4, 2, and 1. The zone tracks are used in combination with the numerical tracks to indicate letters. In this code, for every column, the total spots add to an even number. If for a column the total of the spots in the zone and numerical tracks is an odd number, a spot is added at track *C*.

It is appropriate to state at this point that an electronic system is not infallible. Therefore, it checks itself to find any error. The impulses on channel *C*, or "check," of the tape are used for this purpose. For example, every transfer of information from the memory units might be tested on an odd-even basis. If the sum of the group of digits is an odd number when it is supposed to be even, the machine indicates the error and stops. This is all done automatically by the machine.

The use of magnetic tape as an input medium is further demonstrated by the availability of a hand-operated, portable, magnetic tape digital recorder. Use of this recording machine eliminates the need for punched cards and paper tape for data acquisition and processing. In the case of inventory taking, for example, the bin number, quantity, and material or reference number are recorded on the magnetic tape. Subsequently this tape is fed into the computer, the data processed, and inventory reports printed. The unit has found favor with public utility companies for meter reading. The account or meter number and the reading are recorded by the door to door meter reader. When the tape is filled, it is sent to the computer center where statements to customers, account lists, and reports are prepared. The recording unit is battery powered and handles different sizes of tape cartridges. The maximum cartridge holds about 400 feet of tape. The unit records serially 15-decimal digits per block, a feature which is helpful in attaining error free data collecting.

INFORMATION INTERCHANGE

These are strong efforts being made to adopt a permutation code whereby all coded information could be interchanged between business machines and computers. To this end the American Standards Association has assisted in developing a standard code which is all-inclusive and provides room for future standardization programs. Figure 70 shows this standard code. Its adoption is voluntary by business machine manufacturers, but no doubt it will gradually and surely be utilized. At the same time, the older codes will continue, due to their existence in present machines and to preferences by certain customers for no change.

MAGNETIC TAPE LEDGER RECORD

This medium consists of magnetic strips imbedded on the back side of a ledger record. It serves as a dual-purpose record that is readable by

b7				0	0	0	0	1	1	1	1
b6				0	0	1	1	0	0	1	1
b5				0	1	0	1	0	1	0	1
b4	b3	b2	b1								
0	0	0	0	NULL	DC0	b̶	0	@	P		
0	0	0	1	SOM	DC1	!	1	A	Q		
0	0	1	0	EOA	DC2	"	2	B	R		U
0	0	1	1	EOM	DC3	#	3	C	S		N
0	1	0	0	EOT	DC4 (STOP)	$	4	D	T		A S
0	1	0	1	WRU	ERR	%	5	E	U	U N	S
0	1	1	0	RU	SYNC	&	6	F	V	N A S	G
0	1	1	1	BELL	LEM	' (APOS)	7	G	W	S I G	N E
1	0	0	0	FE0	S0	(	8	H	X	G N	D
1	0	0	1	HT SK	S1	)	9	I	Y	N E	
1	0	1	0	LF	S2	*	:	J	Z	E D	
1	0	1	1	VTAB	S3	+	;	K	[	D	
1	1	0	0	FF	S4	, (COMMA)	<	L	\		ACK
1	1	0	1	CR	S5	-	=	M	]		(1)
1	1	1	0	SO	S6	.	>	N	↑		ESC
1	1	1	1	SI	S7	/	?	O	←		DEL

Courtesy: American Standards Association, Inc., New York
This material is reproduced from the American Standard Code for Information Interchange, X3.4–1963, copyright 1963 by ASA, copies of which may be purchased from the American Standards Association at 10 East 40th Street, New York, N.Y., 10016.

FIG. 70. The standard code for information interchange among information-processing and communications systems. It consists of eight columns of
sixteen characters each. Control characters occupy the first two columns,
punctuation the third, numbers the fourth, alphabet the fifth and sixth. The last
two columns are unassigned, being reserved for future standardization.

machine and by people. Ordinary typing of information on the front side
is translated into computer language on the magnetic strips of the same
ledger record. The strips are capable of storing a large variety of
information. Normally, one of the strips is for positioning purposes prior
to an entry being made on the ledger record; the remaining strips contain
data, some in what is called a positive coding, some in just the opposite, or
negative, code. The positive and negative codes are used for verification
purposes and to insure accuracy. An illustration of the magnetic tape
ledger record is shown in Figure 71.

Courtesy: Burroughs Corp., Detroit

FIG. 71. A magnetic tape ledger record.

The advantages of this medium are unique. They include unlimited access to external memory and to familiar, hard-copy accounting data. Also, simultaneous access to both electronic and human language is provided, thus eliminating separate searching operations. Instructions to the machine can be stored on the magnetic tape ledger records along with human language instructions on the front side, thus expediting the handling and processing work. Changes in instructions are easy to make. In addition, the stored information on the magnetic tape is introduced into the machine as needed, or on a random access basis, thus permitting greater processing flexibility and more utility of the internal memory of the computer for processing.

MAGNETIC INK CHARACTERS

Information can be printed with magnetic ink on ordinary paper. This serves as a medium that can be read by either man or machine. As of the mid-1960's, this medium has been popular for bank checks and deposit slips but has not as yet been extensively adopted for other types of paper work. Study is being given to the extension of magnetic ink to business documents other than checks and deposit slips.

Many are of the opinion that in the near future magnetic ink characters will provide the best means yet devised for automating single documents. The plan is to install an Encoder, which imprints the proper digits, at each point where a charge form, internal debit or credit, and the like are created. Thus, the documents themselves are made the input data, and the need for punching cards or perforating tape is eliminated. The imprinting is such that transit, routing, account number, and amount can be included. Studies indicate the cost would be only about 25 percent that of other appropriate means.

With reference to bank checks the magnetic ink character numerals and characters are the same style and size for all checks. The information conveyed by these imprints is utilized in processing the check in its

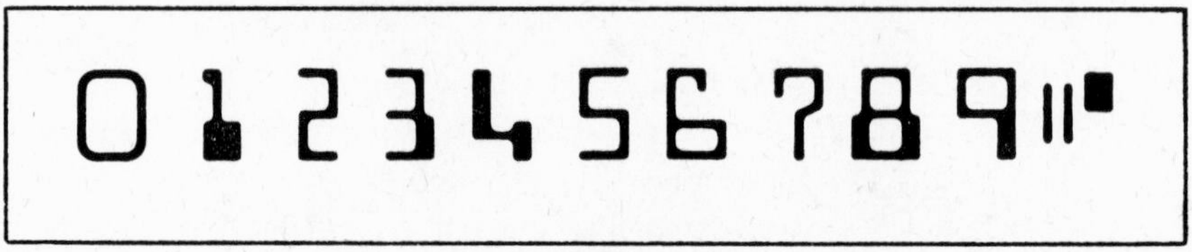

Courtesy: Moore Business Forms, Inc., Niagara, N.Y.

FIG. 72. Type font selected for magnetic ink characters. It can be read visually and also provides optimum machine readability.

journey back to its maker, with the proper bank and individual account being debited or credited. The printing is done with an ink containing iron oxides which are electronically charged and read by magnetic ink character-reading equipment. A special type of design is used in order that the characters can be read visually and maximum machine readability is provided. The printing type employed is of a style called "Font E–13B" and is illustrated by Figure 72. The characters are located on the bank documents in specific areas, such as definite distances from the bottom and right edge, in order that the machines may perform automatically and not have to search for the data.

SPECIAL IMPRINTS FOR MACHINE READERS

There are machines that can do what you are doing right now—reading. A machine reader can read letters and numbers without the use of special ink. Research has demonstrated that to the machine, ordinary printing may be difficult to read because of the variations in normal printing quality. Hence, certain printing type faces resembling conventional type facings have been developed to counter typical printing shortcomings and to meet better the needs of the machine reader. However, the machine can read most printed type, but special imprints are preferred because they give better results. At their present stage of development, most commercially feasible machines are required to read within a relatively small area of the document. It may be an account number, an amount to be paid, or a name and address or a Zip Code number. In the near future, machines to read a page of typed material probably will be available and, beyond that, perhaps a machine to read handwritten material.

Figure 73 shows a machine reader. This particular machine reads a

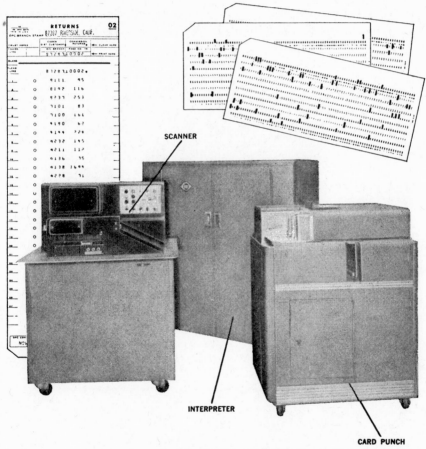

Courtesy: Farrington Electronics, Inc., Needham Heights, Mass.

FIG. 73.   A machine that reads. The unit on the left is the scanner or reader; the center unit, an interpreter; the unit on the right, a card punch machine.

varying number of lines from a printed listing and translates these data into punched cards which are fed into a computer. The machine reader of this type actually does two operations: (1) reads and (2) translates what it reads into computer language. In short, the machine performs human reading and eliminates the laborious manual punching required to prepare punched cards or perforated tapes when used as the input medium. Manufacturers of the reader state that when three or more operators are continuously employed in reading and punching, the machine reader is to be preferred.

Being very versatile, the machine reader can be used for the input of data in many different applications. Credit invoices, checks, order cards, and bill stubs of public utility companies are among the more common uses. Its main areas of application can be classified under two groups: (1) where the input information consists of a long number of separate units recorded in a great number of places and must be processed quickly and economically, and (2) where the output data of today becomes the input data of tomorrow. To illustrate, if a statement with a stub consisting of printed material only is sent to a customer who subsequently returns payment and the stub, it is feasible to put critical portions of the printed matter of the stub in a form that the machine reader can easily handle when the stub is returned and becomes input data.

CHAPTER EIGHT

COMPUTERS—MANAGERIAL

CONSIDERATIONS

*A man's work is in danger of deteriorating when he
thinks he has found the best formula for doing it.*
—Eugene O'Neill

THE REAL potential and future of computers for business data processing
is up to the members of management. Computers enhance the functions of
management; they do not replace it. Computers call for better utilization
of the managerial mind, better managerial actions, and better managerial
accomplishments. Significant improvements in management are possible
by use of the computer, but managers must be truly objective and honest
with themselves if they are to gain the benefits which the computer can
bring about. It is erroneous to think that depositing a modern computer in
the midst of inept management policies, outmoded practices, and an
archaic organization will somehow or other cause corrective miracles to
take place.

The awe-inspiring electronic computers, with their fantastic accomplishments, have led some to refer to them as machines that think. This is
not true. The machines do not think. They operate only as instructed and
must be told what to do in the minutest detail. Decision making is not
their prerogative, except that decision making given to them, which
usually includes modifying their own instructions as dictated by progres-
sive stages of their data processing. Managers, not computers, use their
own judgment and their sense of discrimination. Human beings alone have
intelligence, in that they make free decisions based on a personal value
system. The computer has no value system because it does not have a
mind of its own. This means that managers must still think; they cannot
turn this vital requirement over to the computer. The simplification and
improvement in computer operation have given rise to some erroneously

calling a computer a thinking mechanical human being. It is mechanical, all right; but it is not thinking, and it is not a human being.

MANAGEMENT AND THE COMPUTER

What computers actually do is increase the power and the influence of the human mind, not minimize its importance. They provide help never before believed possible or even conceived. Instead of being overburdened with the processing of data, the human mind can be relieved of such mental drudgery and concentrate its efforts and attention to create, to plan, to ponder and reflect about information, to decide what should be done and whom to inspire. Guesses, hunches, and risks in decision making can be minimized; and decision making on facts and adequate, usable information can be maximized.

Computers increase the responsibility of managers. With the assistance given by computers, the human mind can soar to new heights of accomplishment and acquire knowledge and judgment not yet imagined. The computer can show the way to greater progress, but the accomplishment of hoped-for outputs and gains are regulated by the person issuing the instructions to the computer or figuring out how the computer can be utilized to do what he wants it to do. The potential lies with the manager, not with the moronic metal monster. In essence, computers are tools to be exploited by managers. The challenge is not to be satisfied with the processing of data as such, but to initiate new and revolutionary applications and concepts which are made possible by the use of computers. This necessitates management thinking of the highest order.

THE COMPUTER AND THE OFFICE MANAGEMENT PROCESS

The computer's effect upon management can probably best be seen by considering its effect upon each of the four fundamental functions of management, namely, upon planning, controlling, organizing, and actuating. The office management process affects and, in turn, is affected by the computer. How the manager can best profit by the opportunities made available by the computer and, in turn, how he can best meet the challenges provided by the computer may be approached most effectively from the viewpoint of the office management process. Under planning, for example, we can ask, "What changes in planning are in order due to the availability of the computer?" "Is the technique and scope of planning being modified by computer utilization?"

THE COMPUTER AND MANAGEMENT PLANNING

The scope of planning is usually broadened when the possible use of the computer is considered. More activities can be included, the parameters can be pushed back, and a far more inclusive picture of what makes up the totality of the office work can be included. Actually there should be no restricted areas in the initial development stages of computer usage. Compromises can always be made later, but beginning with circumscribed areas inevitably means ending with restricted areas. The usual pattern in the application of a computer is to a smaller range of activities than was initially considered. Seldom can the best results be achieved by confining it to predetermined limits of activities or to certain organizational limits. Computer work commonly cuts across conventional lines originally established for nonautomated purposes.

In planning for computer utilization, an important and initial consideration is to improve existent systems, procedures, and methods, combining reports, records, and office forms wherever possible, and to point the entire effort toward handling only information that is truly essential. It is folly to put into the computer work that you know is unnecessary. Much of this improvement effort can be made by company personnel; but in many cases, the services of a consultant experienced in this area can save much time and direct the work to a satisfactory conclusion. However, excessive reliance upon outside assistance, particularly from manufacturers of computers, may prove unwise. In the first place this is really not the manufacturer's representative's responsibility. Frequently he is neither familiar with the specific and detailed needs of the company nor aware of the human problems confronting company personnel should the decision to use a computer be made. He can and does render valuable assistance in helping the prospect become more aware of what the equipment can do and the possible aids it can provide.

Adequate planning will avoid the establishment of unrealistic deadlines for the changeover. Frequently, it requires more time to get the computer in operation than is at first realized. The usual pattern is pressure for early installation after long delay in trying to decide whether to install it. Planning helps establish practical schedules and ties together the various required activities into a coordinated program.

THE COMPUTER AND MANAGEMENT CONTROLLING

Periodic follow-up of a computer installation to smooth out operating difficulties is a must. There usually are a number of such difficulties. The follow-up should also include the comparison of "before and after" achievements. By this means areas requiring managerial attention are identified and remedial action is applied to them.

Computer utilization is commonly of a multiproject nature, and this fact emphasizes the importance of establishing effective progress-reporting techniques and carefully monitoring them in order to maintain proper control over each project. Effective reporting techniques are simple, comprehensive, and easy for either the technical or the nontechnical employee to understand. To maintain the support of top management members, it is a good practice to provide them with clear, concise, and up-to-date reports which reveal how each project is progressing and to what extent established goals are being attained.

Job completion dates must be realistic and adhered to; otherwise, control efforts become dissipated. Failure to provide sufficient lead time and allowances for unexpected contingencies is a common cause of establishing completion dates that cannot be fulfilled. The delay of one project aggravates the entire program because work scheduling for a computer closely interrelates all projects within the system. As a result, certain projects may be subjected to completion on a "crash basis," which usually means higher costs and extra follow-up efforts.

THE COMPUTER AND MANAGEMENT ORGANIZING

For genuine success, the various accomplishments of a computer must be integrated with the operational activities of the company. The computer should not be regarded as a new, mysterious entity separated from the main body of the company or as an interesting, captive consulting facility. To achieve the needed integration between information and action functions, it is essential that those working directly with the computer have a clear understanding of their relationships with members in other units of the company and that the authority of the computer personnel be clearly defined. This brings up questions of organization.

Initially, a common practice was to place the computer in the controller's office. Reasons for this varied, but it was thought that this provided a logical organizational location and was an ideal spot for the computer to prove itself a valuable asset. If not in the controller's office, the computer was quite likely to be located somewhere in the finance department. Recent surveys reveal that currently three out of four computers are the responsibility of the financial executive. In some instances data processing has been moved up in the organization; in others it has been relocated. Quite a number feel that the computer should occupy a separate organizational unit and that the manager in charge should report to the president. This arrangement not only accords great importance to office automation, but it also permits a broad scope of operation and a cutting across traditional organizational boundaries, considerations which probably are necessary for a truly integrated information-processing system to exist.

Organization and office automation give rise to the question: "Should centralization or decentralization be followed?" The situation is primarily whether to have (1) a single large installation to serve the office needs of the various operating units of a big enterprise or (2) a number of smaller facilities, each designed and located to serve the needs of one or several of the company's various operating units. The decision depends upon many factors, including the physical size of the enterprise, the total volume of work, the uniformity of work, and the investment required for the equipment.

From the organizational viewpoint, there is also the task of determining clearly the authority and responsibility assigned to those in charge of the computer. Likewise, each subgroup of the computer unit needs to know how it is to work with other groups and the particular duties that it is expected to carry out. In too many companies this organizational relationship has been permitted to become established mainly on an empirical basis, without proper definition of the authority and responsibility of those in charge of this specialized work.

THE COMPUTER AND MANAGEMENT ACTUATING

With all the glamour now being associated with the new office technology, it is easy to forget that people are still vital to office management and will continue to be so. It requires people to operate and maintain computers, and it requires people to interpret and utilize the information made available to them. Successful computer usage requires effective managerial actuating.

The adoption of a computer poses the problem of manpower displacement. This, in turn, frequently necessitates the establishment of certain policies to cope with the human considerations involved. Such policies may include (1) telling the office automation story as it is developed, so that all employees will know what is going on, (2) terminating the employment of no employee because of the new machine—normal attrition will take care of any excess, (3) reducing the salary of no employee because of the computer, and (4) changing job content with reassignment, retraining being provided.

Employees to be affected by the change should be encouraged to participate in designing the change. Normally, this practice brings favorable results. Not only are excellent suggestions offered, but by this practice a needed sense of belonging and importance are enjoyed by the employee. High employee participation usually means high employee cooperation. However, it is a mistake to bypass employees in the planning stages and initially invite them to be a part of the program at the time of installation.

It must be remembered that with the passage of time people tend to become more ready to accept change. The attitude toward office changes almost always becomes more favorable several months after completion of the planning and installation periods than it had been during these periods. People tend to adjust to their surroundings. Experience with new work methods usually demonstrates that many of the fears and unpleasantnesses believed associated with the change actually do not exist or are of much less importance than originally conceived.

Properly handled, the computer system becomes a means of office work that is easier and more practical than any former way. Generally, employees will like the computer way; success or failure depends in large measure upon the quality of actuating efforts performed. The installation should be employee-oriented, not computer-oriented. In the final analysis, the new method is dependent upon the good will, understanding, and cooperation of the employees. To ignore the personnel considerations is certain to invite disaster.

MAJOR COMPUTER USES

Computers provide better information with respect to both quality and quantity. The various uses of computers are many, but for purposes here can be segregated into five major categories: (1) decision making, (2) controlling, (3) simulating, (4) designing, and (5) specific processing of data. The great majority of computer applications can be classified under one or more of these categories.

In the usual sense of the word, decision making can be considered to mean the selecting from possible problem solutions or courses of action, giving due consideration to the objectives and available information. This concept is quite broad and includes both strategic and operating information and whether actions taken should be on a continuous, periodic, or occasional basis. When computers are utilized, the decision making can be either (1) a programmed and routine type, usually featuring measurable quantities; or (2) a programmed but nonroutine type, where the information is restricting and interpretation is emphasized. For the former, typical decision-making examples are those dealing with such things as the quantity of a product to produce next month or an operating budget for a forthcoming fiscal period. For the latter, representative are decisions concerning the products to be included in a product line, and those relating to level of customer service to be provided to compete successfully. To decide these latter types of questions, information is needed and the computer will supply it. But the information must be studied and interpreted in order to arrive at the decision.

When a computer is used for controlling purposes, the facts about what has taken place are put into the machine, in order to obtain specific performance measurements; these values are compared to information showing what is desired; and the respective differences reveal the areas in which corrective action is to be taken. Information on cost, inventory, production runs, and quality of raw materials is illustrative of control material.

Simulating, as pointed out in Chapter 1, is the testing of numerous operating plans to determine the most productive plan. Frequently, but not always, the plans are expressed in mathematical form. However, in all instances, the data must be of a measurable type. In aircraft research, for example, computers are used to simulate different flights for jets. Such factors as allowable pay load, fuel consumption, and speed can be determined accurately without even putting the plane in the air. Likewise by means of a computer, advertising agencies can determine the best combination of media for a particular advertising campaign. The computer is used to try out hundreds of different media combinations and thus reveal the one which maximizes the particular qualities that are being sought. To duplicate manually the information of many combinations would be extremely costly and time consuming. In one such experiment, it required a four-man crew three months to duplicate what the computer provided in six minutes.

A fourth category of computer application is designing. By this is meant the confirmation or rejection of an intelligent guess or hypothesis by the results obtained from carefully directed experimentation. The characteristics of each guess are calculated and checked against specifications. The computer performs these calculations very rapidly. A wide range of possibilities can be considered by the designer; and as a result, the best possible design is identified and used.

Computers are also employed for what may best be termed specific processing of data. This includes the preparation of bank checks, bills, inventory records, and reports of various types. To justify a computer for this work, there usually must be a relatively large volume of work requiring considerable calculating, sorting, or comparing. Otherwise, available machines designed especially to perform the particular work will provide entirely satisfactory results at lower costs.

ADEQUACY OF PRESENT INFORMATION SYSTEM

A fundamental consideration in determining whether to use a computer is the adequacy of the present information system. Many office executives feel that the first move is a thorough analysis of the present means of work performance in order to spot any weaknesses and to determine any foreseeable inability of the present information system to cope with probable future needs. In addition, the possibilities for improving the present information system should be investigated. In many cases, study brings to light hidden potentials within the existing setup. Taking advantage of these opportunities and improving the present system may adequately fulfill the requirements. A chemical manufacturer found that certain revisions and additions in his current conventional way of processing papers would result in substantial savings, and that the use of a computer was possible but would necessitate a high overhead burden and relatively expensive operating payments.

Adequacy is relative and depends upon what is to be accomplished. When considering the use of a computer most companies want to achieve a savings in clerical cost; a capacity to handle increasing work volume; greater accuracy and uniformity in data processing; the securing of better information in less time; better information upon which to base decisions, including the means to enable the technique of either simulation or design to be employed; and improved service to customers. These objectives are not mutually exclusive, but the selection and weight given to each helps formulate the concept of the ideal computer installation from the viewpoint of the particular company.

The volume of transactions is commonly a deciding factor. Computers handle tremendous work volumes within extremely short periods. When a company is faced with an increasing volume of accounts to be processed, the signal for computer utilization may be at hand. This is especially true when the current noncomputer equipment has limited capacity and prohibits procedural refinement and expansion to more mechanization.

Speed of processing is another important consideration. Reference is commonly made to speed as an outstanding gain in the use of computers. It may be vital, but more often than is the case, speed of processing should be considered in relation to service required. To know that with a computer, information for a report can be completed in two hours, in contrast to four days under the present setup, is convincing, provided the report will be used in two hours and will not be ignored or filed away for four days before any use is made of it. The challenge here is to get management members to improve their usage of the material made available. Perhaps this starts with more rapid processing to make information available more quickly and hence more up to the minute.

In addition, speed of processing may directly influence the company's standard of service in comparison with that of its competitors. When an advantage in service is keenly sought, the computer should be evaluated to determine how much its contribution in speed and service will mean in sales and in customer relations.

Some have reasoned, and admittedly with justification, that the computer industry is in its infancy. The future holds improvements and opportunities for computer applications far above any present usage envisioned. The potential is vast. Companies have ordered and installed computers even though studies indicated an operating loss from them for a number of years. But these decisions were reached because it was recognized that some pioneering with a tool as powerful as a computer is probably necessary, that usage begets further usage with the discovery of new applications, and that firsthand experience gained in the use of computers helps to reap the benefits of computerization. However, it is possible to "go overboard" in deciding such issues and wind up in a precarious managerial position.

BATCH OR REAL-TIME?

An important managerial decision regarding computer application is whether batch or real-time process scheduling will be used. Under the former means, all incoming computer data are batched or allowed to accumulate and then processed on a scheduled basis, perhaps once a week. In contrast, for the real-time means data are entered into the computer as soon as available and processed immediately. When real-time is used and the computer is "on-line" with the activity being performed, the expression "on-line real-time" is used.

There is no uniformity of opinion as to when a computer arrangement is precisely real-time. Some contend only control applications are real-time because in these applications processing takes place while the related physical manufacturing operations take place. Others give the term broader meaning and include many types of application where the stored information can be removed at random—called "random access"—in contrast to "serial" types of stored data, which must be removed from the computer in the order of their input. The decision on this issue rests with the individual company. How quickly are the processed data wanted? Letting a customer know within five days of order placement when shipment will be made may be entirely satisfactory, and a batch arrangement would be used. On the other hand, information for a seat reservation on an airplane usually requires a real-time arrangement. At the present stage of progress, most payroll, accounts payable and receivable, cost, and sales analyses are on a batch arrangement, but with the development of systems and the movement toward integrating them, the real-time arrangement could well increase significantly in adoption.

MANAGER-COMPUTER TECHNICIAN RELATIONSHIP

The computer can be a source of controversy between the technician, who knows precisely what the computer can do, and the manager, who can put what it can do to work. It frequently happens that the technician isn't familiar with the manager's needs and, in turn, the manager doesn't understand the technician and is suspicious of the computer because of its far-reaching and revolutionary potential. These divergent viewpoints can be brought together or at least minimized to an appreciable degree. To this end several suggestions are in order.

First, basic policies should be settled before details of the computer utilization are worked out and applied. Computers can open the door to great savings and service opportunities, but to gain them it is necessary and desirable to adjust, delete, and add policies so that the advantages of these opportunities can be won. Almost always needed are statements specifying who is responsible for what decisions, who exercises the prescribed controls, and what the "ground rules" are.

Second, the type of decisions for which the computer will be used should be spelled out. A common practice is to have computer participation in all decisions. This is not only unnecessary but it is also unwise. Too many technicians and specialists get into the act. A simple decision is expanded all out of proportion to its importance. The manager becomes more confused and frustrated. Computers are to assist managers in making better *big* decisions. And our approaches and practices to computer usage should allow the manager and the computer to work together closely.

Also, as pointed out above, computers influence organization and the jobs within it. In some instances the influence results in major modifications; sooner or later there is always some change. Setting forth what these changes probably will be, who will be affected by them and why, tends to smooth the path of application and helps promote good manager-computer technician relationships.

Furthermore, adjustments in long-standing practices assist in acquiring harmonious relationships. Included in the types of popular changes made are (1) elimination of many special files; (2) greater degree of centralized filing; (3) use of "centless accounting"; (4) uniform "days in period" for comparable reports; (5) more data retained on previous functions, such as sales, costs, and collections, to provide helpful trends or comparisons with current data; and (6) greater availability of pertinent data to lower levels of management. In addition, periodic reviews of current computer applications help to uncover other uses and take advantage of available computer time. This state of affairs seems to exist no matter how carefully and thoroughly the initial feasibility study was conducted.

Lastly, the manager should be given basic facts concerning computers and their operation and, likewise, the technician should acquire knowledge of the enterprise and its management. In a sense this is a plea for empathy and, once accomplished, will assist amazingly in acquiring better manager-technician relationships. Mastery of the other's specialty is neither needed nor recommended, but an appreciation and understanding by each of what the other is trying to do, and how he is trying to do it, is mandatory.

PHYSICAL REQUIREMENTS AND TASKS OF CONVERSION

For computer usage, it is usually necessary to provide nonvarying, disturbance-free electrical power and office space that is regulated as to temperature, dust, and humidity. The layout of the office may have to be changed to place the heavy machine where ample structural support is provided and the flow of office work can most efficiently be handled. Channels under the floor in which to run electrical cables connecting the various units sometimes pose a technical problem, especially when a controlling factor is the maximum lengths of cable specified by the computer manufacturer.

Converting large amounts of written material into language required by the computer can represent a herculean task and too often is brushed off as a minor consideration in a computer installation. Conversion difficulties include inaccuracy and lack of uniformity in existing records, missing papers, unexpected deviations of records from a supposed format, errors in reading or in putting information on tape, the maintenance of an adequate work force to accomplish the conversion work, and the accomplishment of the work within reasonable budget limitations.

The conversion process must also take into account what is known as "application in parallel." This means the practice of continuing the processing of information in the normal way and also through the computer, then comparing the results in order to check the accuracy of the computer program. Normally, the work is run in parallel for several complete cycles, or until the new process is completely "debugged." This can be a very frustrating period. Consistent results are obtained; and then, without warning, inconsistencies occur. Finding and correcting the sources of errors frequently pose major tasks. In some installations, conversion problems are minimized by beginning with areas that are already using punched cards or have been subjected to a certain amount of office mechanization, but there is no guarantee that this approach will eliminate conversion difficulties.

COMPUTER ECONOMICS

Excluding scientific and military applications, computers are normally used for the direct savings they effect. Savings in clerical payroll of 15–25 percent and in inventory cost of 15 percent are not unusual. In addition to cost savings, other advantages are sought or effected. These include improved customer service, better control over the operation of the enterprise, and increased speed and accuracy in processing data.

As is true for most machines, the larger and more expensive a computer, the lower the unit cost per processing operation. The greater capacity, speed, and versatility of the big computer make its unit cost relatively low. To illustrate, the huge IBM STRETCH computer, with a high usage rate, will perform 100,000 calculations for only 2½ cents. Or this computer will do for less than $1 what it would cost $10 to do on a small computer or perhaps $8,000 with an ordinary desk calculator. Volume and type of work are the key factors.

Three choices are available to the user of a computer: he can (1) buy the computer, (2) rent the computer, or (3) hire a computer service. The cost differs for each of these conditions. With purchase there is a large capital expenditure plus an annual expenditure for operation and maintenance. Rental entails a much smaller expenditure, with standard expenses for operation. Commonly the rental represents about one-third of the total annual operating costs. To hire a computer service requires no capital, operation, or maintenance costs, but a fee for the work performed.

Currently, the rental or lease arrangement represents approximately 80 percent of computer installations. Usually rental agreements contain an option to buy, but few of these options are exercised. Rental or computer service may be favored if there is uncertainty of forecast in computer usage. Also, the small computer user may not be able to justify hiring and training a maintenance crew, which he can avoid by rental or hiring a computer service. Expensive programming for specialty work usually can be minimized by using the computer service. On the other hand, lower net cost in the long run may point to the purchase of the computer as the best decision. The federal government uses a *cost advantage point* in determining whether to buy or lease. This is the point when purchase price plus accrued maintenance equals cumulative rentals for a particular computer.

When this point is reached in six years or less, purchase is warranted providing it appears that the computer will meet the job requirements without major modifications. Limited research indicates that it usually takes around six years for computer investment to be recovered. Low point in recovery is the end of two or three years, due primarily to the effect of start-up costs, changeover, and adjustments.

Computer service is offered by over 150 U.S. companies who are specialists familiar with all computers. Some are independent companies, others are service bureaus owned or operated by computer manufacturers. Their charges vary according to factors such as type of computer and the amount of work, but generally charges are considered nominal and in line with the services rendered. The services offered by these companies are ideal for excess work loads and where computer usage is occasional.

It can be seen that many considerations can enter into the decision on which of the three alternatives should be chosen. The total cost can vary widely. Cost is probably most important, but it is not the sole consideration. The company's individual requirements and the manager's judgment are equally influential factors. A helpful comparison of the three basic choices is obtained by forecasting the annual total expenses for the most favorable and suitable arrangement for each choice. This can be projected over a reasonable number of years. Such data, along with attention to nontangible considerations, assist in arriving at a decision.

WILL IT PAY TO WAIT?

With a field as dynamic and fast-growing as computers, the question arises: "Will it pay to wait in order to obtain a better buy to fulfill our data-processing needs?" Computers, like any other machine, wear out; but experience to date shows that most electronic equipment functions perfectly even after 10 years of use, and engineering estimates are that a usable life of 20–25 years is reasonable. The usefulness of a computer can be reduced by failure of the unit to meet changed requirements. However, proper planning, taking into account probable future needs for 5 to 10 years, can minimize most of this loss so that it should not become serious. Furthermore, the utilization of computers employing modular-type design that "grow with the user" helps to meet the problem.

Delay in acquiring data-processing equipment might be thought the best decision when consideration is given to the amazing advances made possible by engineering improvements. In the relatively brief history of computers, improvements have been more in the nature of speed, convenience, and capacity rather than in a radically different basic design. Likewise, computers to serve the special needs of a particular industry or type of application have been developed and employed. In many respects, efforts have concentrated on perfecting components which are made available, but certainly not mandatory, to existing systems. Seldom do these components make the rest of the system obsolete. In the case of rental units, the newest components, as they become available, are commonly incorporated into the system.

The subject of costs and the payout period raise some interesting considerations in deciding the question of whether to wait or to proceed with a computer installation now. The total period in a projected installation must be considered. It is unrealistic and incomplete analysis to begin with some future date and ignore the interim period from the present to the start of that future period. Savings, if any, should be considered from using what is available today. Displacements of this system by future changes can be taken into account.

The data of Figure 74, while hypothetical, serve to illustrate a

YEAR	PROCESS SYSTEM No. 1		PROCESS SYSTEM No. 2		PROCESS SYSTEM No. 1 AND No. 2	
	Yearly	Cumulative	Yearly	Cumulative	Yearly	Cumulative
1	− 50	− 50			− 50	− 50
2	− 65	−115			− 65	−115
3	− 70	−185	− 50	− 50	−120	−235
4	+105	− 80	− 70	−120	+ 15	−220
5	+ 90	+ 10	− 75	−195	+ 75	−145
6	+100	+110	+100	− 95	+150	+ 5
7	+100	+210	+100	+ 5	+160	+165
8	+110	+320	+110	+115	+175	+340
9	+110	+430	+120	+235	+175	+515
10	+110	+540	+140	+375	+175	+690

FIG. 74.   Loss or savings for each of three different installations of data-processing systems for a ten-year period (in $000,000).

common situation regarding timing and payout period for data-processing systems. Under process system No. 1, a net saving appears in the fifth year, with total savings at the end of ten years being $540,000. Process system No. 2 illustrates waiting until a new machine is on the market and installing it in the third year. Under this arrangement, total savings at the end of the tenth year are $375,000, not as favorable as under process system No. 1, but toward the end of the period increasing yearly at a faster rate than those of system No. 1. However, if system No. 1 is started in the first year and converted to the improved machine, and system No. 2 in the third year, the cumulative savings amount to $690,000, a sizable increase over either those of system No. 1 or those of No. 2 used singly.

In addition, it should be pointed out that the initial conversion to a computer system involves a great deal of work and time. But it is highly probable that the second conversion necessitated by adopting process systems No. 1 and No. 2 will be relatively far less difficult due to previous experience and that the second conversion will stress "debugging" the new system rather than the physical work involved in converting to the new system.

THE COMPUTER SELECTION

It has been customary to appoint a committee to select the computer. Normally this gives very satisfactory results. The ideal committee consists of experienced managers, preferably from the upper organizational levels. This group can be supplemented by another group representative of the major areas to be affected by the installation of the computer. In some instances, a committee has been used to carry out the work of studying the status of the present information system; and when this practice is followed, the same committee continues to serve in the selection of the type of computer.

Knowledge about various computers must be acquired by the committee members; and this is best done by attending schools offered by the computer manufacturers, reading available literature on the subject, and conferring with executives of companies having computers in operation. After a period of several months, an effort is made to determine what types of work should be done by a computer and what type of computer appears best for the company's present and reasonable future needs.

Competent consultants can be employed to give assistance in drawing up recommendations pertaining to the company's work to be done on a computer, the type of machine, steps in application, and pitfalls to be avoided in these efforts. The consultant's wide and varied experience can save much time and spark the action to move ahead. But participation by the company personnel is essential, for it provides them with practical insight as to what is going on and why. Furthermore, familiarity with the proposed processing is gained, and the background needed for successful installation and operation is obtained.

The use of a committee can assist in attaining a unified program of preparation and installation. Important groups such as the systems and procedures department, the personnel department, and the departments in which changes will occur can be represented on such a committee. Planning pertaining to the feasibility of automation—the how, when, and where of the changes to be made; and the means for handling these changes, especially with reference to personnel—can be handled quite successfully by a committee.

A number of criteria can be used in the task of selecting a particular computer. Among the more common are (1) completion of operations within a fixed time, (2) cost, (3) the most versatile computer within a given maximum expenditure, (4) specific computer features, (5) proven performance, and (6) the manufacturer. Under this latter consideration, such bases as experience in computer manufacturing, installation and training service, and caliber of maintenance service usually rank high.

COMPUTER CENSUS

Since 1951, when the U.S. Bureau of the Census installed the first large electronic data-processing system for business data, nearly 20,000 systems have been put into operation. This estimate is for general-purpose systems; it does not reflect specialized installations, as in banks, except in the case of the larger banks where large general-purpose systems are in use. Included in this estimate are the small or desk-size computers, which have opened up a number of users with relatively limited amounts of data processing to be handled. Governmental sources reveal that the number of computers in federal government use as of June, 1965, was nearly 750.

Arbitrary classifications by size of computer system are sometimes followed, including (1) large, (2) medium, and (3) small. Such classifications are actually very broad and rough. The classification "large" includes computer systems renting for over $30,000 monthly. These represent the sophisticated systems with top speeds and special features. "Program interrupt," for example, will usually be included in the abilities of this group. This is the ability of the computer to accept instructions simultaneously by selecting an input or output device ready to join the processing and start this processing at the same time other input and output devices are completing their functions. This raises the "throughput" and assists in conserving valuable processing time. The second group, "medium," constitutes those with rental costs averaging between $5,000–$10,000 monthly. They make up the popular computer systems, widely used and perhaps best known of all computers. Most in this group have mass memory hardware and effective input and output devices. The last group, "small," represents machines renting for around $1,000–$2,000 per month. These have relatively limited capacity but perform satisfactorily within their limits. Punched cards or tape are commonly the input media, tape and printed matter the output media. Many have very limited mass memory, if any, and this condition poses problems in processing, requiring, for example, the referencing of indicative data. Usually the practice is to rely on punched cards or tape for these data as well as the variable data. This results in slower processing, but lower cost.

Figure 75 shows a comparison of computers and highlights certain

Name	Price (Thousands of Dollars)	Average Monthly Rental	Storage Capacity	Media	
				Input	Output
LARGE:					
Control Data 1604-A	$1,200	$37,000	6 million words (D) 32,000 words (C)	K–MT–PC–PT	K–MT–PC–PT–PR
Honeywell 1800	1,650	30,000	1,080 million characters (D) 8–32,000 words (C)	K–MT–PC–PT	K–MT–PC–PT–PR
IBM 7090	3,000	65,000	280 million characters (D) 32,000 words (C)	K–MT–PC–PT	K–MT–PC–PR
RCA 601	2,000	35,000	1 million characters (Dr) 8–32,000 words (C)	K–MT–PT	MT–PR
Univac 1107	2,250	45,000	16–65,000 words (C)	K–MT–PC–PT	MT–PC–PT–PR
MEDIUM:					
Burroughs 200	225	6,000	480 million characters (D) 4–8,000 words (C)	K–MT–PC–PT	MT–PC–PT–PR
Gen. Elec. 210	750	14,000	20 million characters (D)	K–MT–PC–PT	K–MT–PC–PT–PR
IBM 1401	175	4,000	1–16,000 words (C)	MT–PC–PT	PC–PR
NCR 315	250	6,500	10–80,000 words (C)	K–MT–PC–PT	K–MT–PC–PT–PR
SMALL:					
Gen. Prec. LGP-30	50	1,200	4,000 words (C)	K	PR
Monroe Monrobot XI	25	700	1–2,000 words (Dr)	K–PC–PT	PC–PT–PR

CODE: D = Disk   K = Keyboard   PT = Perforated Tape
      C = Core   MT = Magnetic Tape   PR = Printer
      Dr = Drum   PC = Punched Card

FIG. 75. A comparison of computers.

differences among them. For this list the computers were selected arbitrarily, but they do represent many, even though not all, of those in common use. The illustration is intended to be indicative only, not conclusive.

THE COMPUTER AND RETURN ON INVESTMENT

Some managers believe that their computer investments are not giving adequate return on investment. The computers are providing advantages and improvements, but not in the amount and kind that it is believed they should. This condition stems from various causes including limited competency of computer personnel, lack of sufficient top management interest in computer application, and insufficient managerial effort to determine the economic facts of the computer operations. For example, no study is made of the relative importance of the work being processed, computer time is crowded with menial data "just to keep it busy," no formal method is followed for choosing applications, and no estimates or charges are made of what various computer applications are costing. Many managers, in fact, do not know how much their computer is saving or earning; their operation being based to a great degree on faith.

What is needed is the same type of operational analysis applied to computers as is applied to extensive research projects and expensive marketing projects. Specifically, this involves several important steps. First, carefully estimate the potential gains from a proposed computer application. This is not easy. All work performed in the before and after arrangement must be identified, the effect upon corporate resources and cost estimated, and key adjustments required for the changeover evaluated. To ignore these basic requirements may prove tragic. Assuming the popular, "How can we miss?" attitude can lead to serious difficulties. Second, devise a means for measuring the potential benefits. This necessitates not only identifying what they are, but also evaluating their worth. If the benefit is dollars saved, how does this amount compare with the cost of obtaining them? If less time is to be taken, can and will it be used for accomplishing other work? Third, exercise the required control to see that the expected benefits are obtained. No computer controls itself. Managerial control must be applied to its operation in order to insure successful completion of plans designed to bring about the benefits being sought. Fourth, establish a cost system for charging company departments or accounts for computer operations. This helps to fix responsibility and places computer operations on a sound businesslike basis. Here again to establish this practice requires much hard work, but the effort is well worth while. A suggested approach is to (1) determine the present (noncomputer) and proposed (computer) cost of processing the work, (2) charge the original department with the present processing cost, (3) charge the computer department for developing the computer application, and (4) credit the computer department with the savings achieved from the computer application.

SUGGESTIONS FOR COMPUTER USERS

Many of the problems of computers must be solved in managers' offices rather than in the laboratories of the designing engineers. Experts in the area of computer installation quickly point out that each installation has its unique difficulties, but certain general practices usually aid in achieving complete satisfaction within a minimum of time. Among the suggestions covering these practices are the following:

1. View the computer as a data-processing system, not as a single machine. See it as a means for supplying information to an enterprise, not as a replacement for a single or particular office machine.

2. Learn as much as possible about the various uses of computers. This knowledge will broaden your viewpoint and assist in maximizing utilization of the computer.

3. Have top managers or a top group decide what work should be done with a computer. Do not permit one involved department head to make this decision.

4. Never consider a computer the cure-all for all current paper work ills. A computer assists in attaining improvements, but employees must improve the system. The computer does what it is told to do.

5. In planning a data-processing system, take into consideration the probable needs for the future 5 to 10 years.

6. Always relate computer capability to the specific requirements of the installation being considered. Capacities and special types of work performed which are not needed by the system at hand are superfluous.

7. With sufficient training, use present personnel for computer operation, as they usually can operate a data-processing system very satisfactorily.

8. Work closely with the computer manufacturer, who is anxious to assist in attaining a completely satisfactory installation.

CHAPTER NINE

COMPUTERIZED OFFICE

APPLICATIONS

*Do not fear to repeat what has already been said. Men
need these things dinned into their ears many times and
from all sides. The first version makes them prick up
their ears, and the second registers and the third enters.*
—*Lenac*

NEW applications of computers are one of the really basic and dynamic
areas of our economy. The list seems almost endless and touches almost
every facet of human activity. In this chapter, some idea of the various
and interesting types of applications will be briefly discussed. Our purpose
is to provide an indication of the part the computer is playing and is
destined to play in the future. Let us start with several concise and
pertinent at random computer applications and follow these with more
detailed discussions of six outstanding applications of computers.

AT RANDOM COMPUTER APPLICATIONS

Can you envision the work involved in preparing the data and writing
nearly 5 million paychecks a month—that's more than 200 thousand per
day. An agency of the federal government is calculating, writing, and
proofing that quantity successfully by means of a computer. In addition,
the computer keeps up-to-date revised addresses, amounts due, and changes
occurring from time to time, so that the information and check writing are
current and correct for each month. Any corrections or changes can be
recomputed by day, month, or year. The computer is practically error-
proof.

In operation in 1967 is a supercomputer capable of internal processing speeds up to 12 times faster than the ordinary large and powerful computer. This supercomputer can perform 8 million additions or 5 million multiplications in one second. It is designed for problems in space exploration, subatomic physics, theoretical astronomy, and global weather forecasting. Its cost is $6 million with peripheral equipment.

By means of computerized typesetting systems, type for book matter and newspaper reading matter and classified advertising from unjustified tape made by electric typewriters is now being produced. The computer justifies the line—makes the right margin even, divides hyphenated words correctly, controls line width, selects type sizes and faces. For newspapers, the handling of wire service copy, including programming of corrections and new leads due to later news, are all handled automatically. In one hour about 12,000 lines of 8-point type in 11-pica column width can be produced. In addition, devices handle the output tape to the completion of the finished galleys of completed type are delivered by the linecasting machines. About 600 lines an hour in this width is the speed of the linecasting machine. Thus, about 20 linecasting machines are required for the automated arrangement.

Computers can now talk. An audio response unit makes information within a computer available over the telephone. Words and sounds are recorded by human voice and stored within the computer. Upon inquiry, the words are assembled to form a verbal answer which is transmitted to the caller. Currently about 30 to 125 words are stored, depending upon the flexibility needed and the specific needs of the business. To illustrate, an employee in a branch insurance office in Seattle can obtain policy information from a company computer on the East Coast by dialing several numbers on the telephone. Seconds later he hears a verbal reply to his inquiry. A large department store in Chicago now utilizes a computer-directed credit authorization system that gives a verbal reply to a salesperson's inquiry in less than 30 seconds. All sales-floor telephones in 12 different stores are hooked to the central computer which can handle 10,000 credit approvals daily. However, the computer's capacity is so large that credit applications use less than 5 percent of its time. Hence, the computer is used to prepare over 6 million customer statements a year, write reminder notices to customers, print sales promotion material, and identify probable bad debt accounts.

Computers can also "televise" information. An installation in a well-known insurance company retains 400 million characters of customer information and displays, almost instantly, a customer's policy records on a television-type screen. To obtain information on any policy, its number is typed on a machine unit attached to the display screen. In less than a second, the required data are obtained from the computer, converted to visual characters, and displayed on the screen. All transactions such as premium payments and changes of address are checked and posted daily against the master file of information. Within a normal working day, 600,000 policyholders' records can be reviewed and updated.

Equally striking is "Sketchpad," the robot draftsman. The face of a television-type display tube is used like a sheet of paper on which sketches are drawn using an electronic stylus. With Sketchpad, the designer can find out how his new mechanical arrangement will perform without building a model. The computer will animate the drawing, calculate stresses at specified locations, duplicate electric circuit diagrams to determine behavior of current flows, and a variety of other information. Thus, the computer is helpful in creative design. Advantages include increased analysis capability which is more complete in both scope and detail than previously attainable. Heretofore the accepted approach was essentially an art in that designs were formulated largely on the basis of experience and trial and error methods. With the computer, however, most of the possible design parameters can be analytically determined, designs formulated, tested, and detailed drawings provided. The results are improved product quality, elimination of prototype developments, enormous savings of design time, and a revolution of an old established technology.

Beginning in 1968, one of the large airlines will use three big integrated computers with a total of nearly 1 billion characters of random access storage. This capacity will permit 100 percent expansion in keeping with projected passenger growth. A total of 700 printer units will provide agents with copy information and operational messages in addition to the visual readout. The computer installation will enable the agent to issue a ticket with confirmed reservations in several seconds. Cost of the total computer installation: $56 million.

No-check banking and no-cash shopping are also realistic. How is this possible? By debits and credits to bank accounts electronically via the telephone. To pay a bill, a consumer simply inserts a card into a special slot at the back of his telephone and dials his bank's computer number. Then he dials the amount of his bill and within seconds is informed by an electronic voice, described in the above paragraph, that the given amount has been transferred from his account into the account of the company he is paying. Separate cards could be used, each for one company that regularly bills the consumer. Or an individual credit card for use anywhere over a wide communication data network could be followed. The "pay by phone" arrangement can also be used for retail transactions by those subscribing to the system. At the supermarket, for example, a customer at the checkout counter produces his credit card instead of cash. The attendant inserts the card into the supermarket-to-bank telephone. What the customer owes is transferred at once from his bank account to the supermarket's account. Are these dreams of computer-minded men? Not at all. These systems are in existence in several experiments, are proving successful, and signal fantastic changes ahead in bank services and credit.

Claims for improving football are also listed among the computer's accomplishments. By viewing a slow-motion film of all plays during a game, each player is rated on a one-to-seven scale. A score of seven is given for a fumble or for being the cause of a penalty. In contrast, intercepting a pass or successfully blocking two opponents rates a top mark of one. Each player's game record is put into the computer where a play-by-play, game-by-game, or season-by-season analysis and blueprint for victory can be developed. The history of a particular formation or pass pattern is revealed; what is successful and what is not, and the best sequence of plays both for offense and for defense are identified and mastered.

COMPUTER GRAPHICS

Our first selected application for more detailed discussion is computer graphics. High-speed two-axis plotting of digital computer output for either on-line or off-line operations is now an accomplished fact. Significant applications include engineering drawings, medical research, stress-strain diagrams, calibration curves, meteorological studies, learning curves, water profiles, harmonic analysis, ray tracing, and PERT. The list of applications is constantly expanding. No longer is it necessary to spend long and tedious hours plotting data into graphic form. The computer will do this for us.

The CALCOMP digital incremental plotter is driven by the computer. Direct coupling frequently can be used, but for the larger computer the signal instructions are received by a medium for subsequent use by the plotter off-line. A special adapter converts the computer output to a form suitable for driving the plotter. Figure 76 shows the versatile, completely automatic high-speed plotting system. The insert in upper left of this illustration shows a close-up of the plotting unit. Values for preparation of a learning curve are being plotted. The completed chart is removed in a manner similar to that of taking a piece of paper from a roll of wrapping paper. Figure 77 illustrates a geologic chart produced

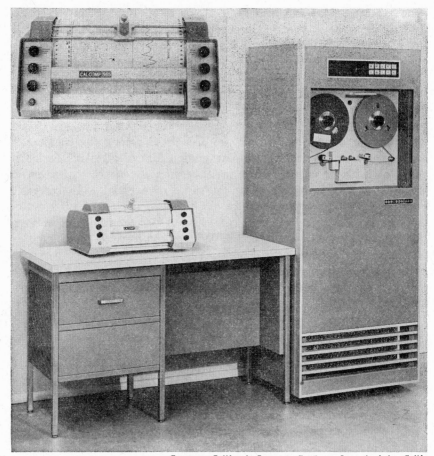

Courtesy: California Computer Products, Inc., Anaheim, Calif.

FIG. 76. A magnetic tape plotting system. Featuring a high-speed automatic search, plotting of continuous curve or points, this unit produces graphs up to 29½ inches wide by 120 feet long.

automatically by CALCOMP plotter from data in a computer. Figure 78 shows a computer-plotter producing a contour map. This unit is applicable to most horizontal geometrical designs including bridge structures, highway designs, and computations for right-of-way projects.

The plotting is produced by movement of a pen relative to the surface of the paper. Each input impulse causes a very minute step, of either .01 inches or .005 inches, on either the X-axis or the Y-axis. A deflection on the X-axis is produced by motion of the drum, on the Y-axis by motion of the pen carriage. Signals raise and lower the pen as required. Each step

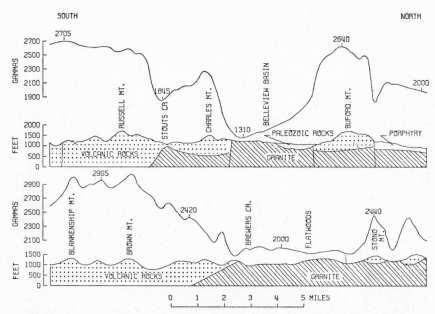

STRUCTURE AND LITHOLOGY FROM AEROMAGNETIC PROFILES OVER THE ST. FRANCOIS MOUNTAINS
Courtesy: California Computer Products, Inc., Anaheim, Calif.

FIG. 77.   Example of chart drawn automatically from data in a computer.

can be in any one of 24 basic step combinations or directions made up of its X and Y values, i.e., the basic step direction for a plotted point can be any of 24 directions within the 360-degree quadrant made up of X and Y values of .01 or .005 inches.

INFORMATION RETRIEVAL—AUTOMATICALLY

Much of the money spent for research and development will be spent more effectively or not at all when available literature on the subject can be searched thoroughly beforehand. There are thousands of technical journals carrying literally millions of articles on a vast array of scientific subjects. Screening and retrieving what is pertinent to a particular study represents a herculean task for the searcher. In many cases, research is started on a project already completed or in process elsewhere, or not all the available knowledge has been reviewed before launching the new study.

This gives rise to another facet of office technology, called automatic information retrieval. Succinctly stated, this can be called mechanization of the intellectual effort of information input to provide quick screening of

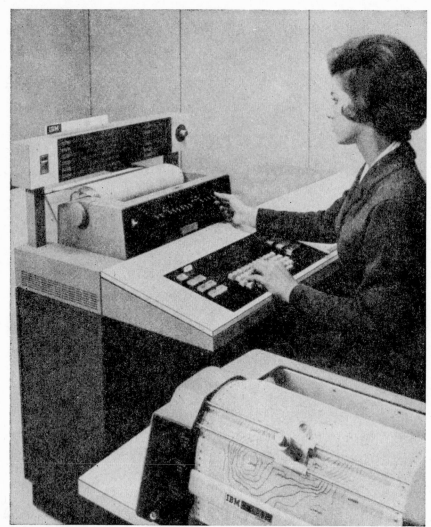

Courtesy: International Business Machines Corp., New York;
and California Computer Products, Inc., Anaheim, Calif.

FIG. 78. Computer and CALCOMP plotter enables engineers to state problems to the computer and receive immediate answers in printed or graphic form.

voluminous available information on any of a multitude of subjects. It is a terrific time consumer, if indeed physically possible, to follow through all the reports and journals to keep pace with developments in a given field of study. The need is for a fast way to have access to information on specific subjects. This, in turn, requires some means by which masses of data are assimilated, classified, and compressed into complete and understandable indexes; and if desired, the complete information itself can be retrieved quickly.

It is estimated that some $1.5 billion are spent each year for research and development, and a goodly portion of this amount goes for "information services" or searching the literature. Much of this can be handled by the use of computers, but it should be pointed out that other mechanical means are possible and in use. For example, a large pharmaceutical house maintains a punched-card index file on 15,000 drug journal articles that goes back five years. Cost for this arrangement is only $550 a month. Other systems use a combination punched card and microfilm, with the latter located within the center portion of the card. The card is used to locate the title and subject, the microfilm for showing a portion or all of a copy of the original article. The microfilm can be projected on a special screen for reading convenience.

Different but closely associated with information retrieval is the belief by many that the computer will help bring about the common world language so long sought. The belief is that as man learns to communicate with machines, this communication will spread to man-to-man communication. Thus, "computerese" may end language barriers. On the other hand, it seems that to eradicate any language of long standing will certainly not be an overnight accomplishment. But communication between men of different languages is an accomplished fact of the computer. It can translate information from one language into another. Such units are feasible, but this application to date has been relatively minor compared to the host of other uses to which computers have been applied.

VISIBLE RECORD—MICR AUTOMATION SYSTEM

Banks can now enjoy the fastest check handling at the lowest cost per item and highest accuracy in banking history. This is made possible by a visible record computer using MICR (magnetic ink character recognition) source documents. This office automation system is specifically designed for financial accounting. Flexible MICR and punched-card inputs are utilized; electronic processing and retention of accounting records in ordinary visual form (printing on paper) are features of this process. The accounting records are maintained on magnetic tape ledger cards which, as pointed out in Chapter 7, are regular-appearing ledger cards with magnetic tape imbedded on the back side of the card. Information typed on the front side is translated into computer language on the magnetic strips of the same card.

The system is made up of four essential units. These are illustrated in Figure 79 and include, viewing from left to right, (1) the sorter-reader, (2) the record processor and console, (3) the card reader, and (4) the data processor. The latter is the nerve center of the entire system. It performs all calculations, gives instructions, and directs the operations of the other three units.

Encoded MICR items—for example, bank checks in the case of our bank illustration—are read and sorted automatically by the sorter-reader unit to provide on-line and buffered data input for the record processor unit. In other words, the check is read regarding such information as the account number, process control number, and amount from the magnetic

Courtesy: Burroughs, Inc., Detroit

FIG. 79.   The essential units of the visible record-MICR automation system.

ink markings on the check and sorted to a batch of checks, which expedites the posting of the transactions to the check writer's account or statement. The sorter-reader processes mixed items of varying sizes and thicknesses at rates of over 1,500 per minute.

The information read by the sorter-reader is transmitted to the record processor and console, which automatically selects from its file of records the desired record by account number, reads the data stored in the magnetic tapes or strips on the back of the account ledger record, updates both the printed side and the magnetic storage area of each currently active record amount, and returns the ledger record to the file. The recording of data is accomplished by means of a printer capable of over 200 lines per minute, each line consisting of 156 characters. The accounting records are filed by batches in the processor, and the record needed for posting is brought to the front part of the unit for posting operations. Those records requiring special attention are segregated by means of an auxiliary unit called a stacker. Three input stations for forms provide operating versatility. The console supplies the means of communicating between the supervisor and the system.

One of the important functions of the card reader is to supply on-line data input to the system from punched cards. It does this at a rate of 200 cards per minute. In addition, this unit puts programs into the core memory of the data processor, input data for selected data-processing applications, and the processing of exceptional items.

The entire system supplies up-to-the-minute information of current status and previous activity for each account. Simultaneous daily printing of the ledger, statement, and journal avoids the end-of-period statement-printing peaks. In addition, vital analysis of the records can be conducted quickly, the records are balanced step by step to insure complete accuracy, and lower operating costs provide better operational control.

PROCESSING PUBLIC UTILITY CUSTOMER ACCOUNTS

The preparation of bills for more than 500,000 electric and gas meters is another interesting application of an electronic data-processing system. Readings from the meter readers' reports are typed on a special report using a machine which simultaneously makes a perforated tape of the information. This tape is fed into the computer, which reads the information at high speed. Being given the customer's number and present meter reading, the computer locates the information it has on the particular customer number; subtracts the previous from the present meter reading; computes the cost and discount, if any; and, along with the customer's name and address, sends the processed information to the output unit, where the customer's bill is printed. Subsequently, the bills are sorted automatically by cities and mail zone numbers for putting in the mail.

The monthly, bill has the customer's account number preprinted in magnetic ink. This number identifies the account. When bill stubs are returned for crediting customer payments, they are sorted by customer number and read by a sorter-reader unit similar to that described above. From this unit, the information is fed into the computer, which posts the payment to customer ledger cards in the form of magnetic tape ledger cards. Approximately 12,000 customer bills are prepared in one hour. It required about one year to complete the switchover to the new system, but this conversion was accomplished without any inconvenience to the customers of the public utility.

New meter installations and changes of address and number of meter are handled in the same manner as the input of monthly billing data. The new meter is assigned a customer's number; or if the case requires, the new address is added, and the old address is removed from the data in the computer's memory units. These additions and changes create extra work. However, initial estimates placed this work at not more than 2,200 per month, whereas the actual requirements have never exceeded 1,720 in any one month. The system does provide needed flexibility as well as great accuracy and speed.

In addition to processing customer accounts, the company intends to use the computer for the handling of engineering computations and studies. This will facilitate design and planning work so essential to the improvement of new electric and gas facilities necessary to meet future requirements. Other areas for future exploration include payroll, accounts payable, property and plant records, and inventory.

INVENTORY CONTROL DATA PROCESSING

Like many applications, the work of inventory control, as it is normally thought of, must be modified so that it is in a form that meets the physical operational requirements of computer handling. In this respect, a common arrangement for inventory control by computer is the cumulative or "cum" system, in which all activity is directed toward the new cum or total quantity. Information can be thought of as being gathered by degrees, and quantities increase in number until the entire records are started again from a new base. In essence, if cum is available, inventory is available at the proper time and in the proper quantity. There is no need for balance-of-stores records common in noncomputer inventory control systems.

An understanding of the basic operations performed is essential for comprehending the working of the inventory control data processing. Hence, before discussing what the computer does, a brief description of the basic operations will be given. The initial step is the sales forecast, which is reviewed monthly and adjusted in light of market conditions. A "release for production" is made against the sales forecast, which release authorizes procurement of materials, production schedules, and final assembly. Comparison is made between the cumulative requirements and the amount available. If the latter exceeds the former, no order for parts is entered. On the other hand, if the amount available is less than the cumulative requirements, the deficit is filled by ordering the parts.

The Data Utilized.   In Figure 80, the top illustration shows that for Model 124, the amount released is 5,000; shipped, 2,400; February scheduled shipment, 1,000; March scheduled shipment, 1,500. Thus, the cum for February is 3,400 and for March, 4,900. The data are converted to weekly amounts, as indicated by the middle illustration of Figure 80. So

Model	To Date		February		March	
	Release	Cum Shipped	Release	Cum Shipped	Release	Cum Shipped
124	5,000	2,400	1,000	3,400	1,500	4,900

FEBRUARY

Week A		Week B		Week C		Week D	
R*	CS*	R	CS	R	CS	R	CS
250	2,650	250	2,900	250	3,150	250	3,400

MARCH

Week A		Week B		Week C		Week D	
R	CS	R	CS	R	CS	R	CS
375	3,775	375	4,150	375	4,525	375	4,900

COMPONENT NO. 1 FOR ALL MODELS

FEBRUARY

Week A		Week B		Week C		Week D	
R	CS	R	CS	R	CS	R	CS
1,500		1,500		1,500		1,500	

MARCH

Week A		Week B		Week C		Week D	
R	CS	R	CS	R	CS	R	CS
1,625		1,625		1,625		1,625	

* R = Release; CS = Cum Shipped.

FIG. 80. Data utilized in "cum" method of inventory control.

far, our data are by model, and each model may require a number of components. Quite probably, some of these components will be common to several models. Our need is to determine the total number of each component that will be required for the scheduled product mix represented by the various models. Assume the monthly data illustrated by the bottom illustration of Figure 80 represent these values. The amounts required will be determined primarily on the sales forecasts of each model, with important modifications for in-plant lead time. This is to say that some components are required for subassemblies, others for the final assembly; those for subassemblies must be available in the plant for consumption before the components intended for final assembly. In many instances, the same type of component will be used for the subassembly and again in the final assembly.

For each component, comparisons are now made between the cum and the availability. Based on this comparison, the decision to "order schedule" is determined. Referring to Figure 81, the cum requirements

COMPONENT NO. 1 FOR ALL MODELS

	Used to Date	February			
		Week A	Week B	Week C	Week D
Cum requirements	13,400	14,900	16,400	17,900	19,400
Available	22,000	22,000	22,000	22,000	22,000
Order schedule		0	0	0	0

FIG. 81.

for component 1 are 13,400 for the "used to date." As indicated in Figure 80, the requirements for the first week of February are 1,500, making the cum 14,900; for the second week, 1,500, making the cum 16,400; and so forth. The availability of component 1 is 22,000, which, compared to the cum of February week A, shows ample supply; hence, no order schedule would be made, and the value of 0 is entered under week A. In like manner, it can be seen that no order schedule for component 1 would be issued during any of the weeks of February. Even the last week shows the cum will be 19,400, with 22,000 available. Production planning is quite unlikely to match exactly sales forecasts because of the varying need for finished goods inventory, variations in estimated lead times, rates of production, and capacity to produce exactly to requirements. But the system provides reasonable checks between weekly needs and availability, so that deviations are kept within practical limits; thus, satisfactory inventory control is achieved.

Automating the Process. This system is suited to automation. It utilizes a computer designed to approach in-line accounting on a mechanized basis. Such a computer is equipped with a random access storage device which permits the storage of and rapid access to any of many millions of characters comprising the records. The various accounts may be posted in random order. For example, interrelated transactions might involve (1) securing raw materials, for which the transaction is posting receipts to raw material record; (2) making up subassemblies, for which the transactions are posting production of subassemblies to subassembly account and deducting components used in subassemblies from components accounts; or (3) shipping finished goods, which requires for the record a deduction from the finished goods account by the amount of finished goods shipped.

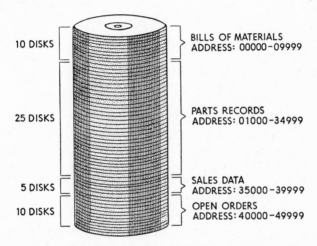

FIG. 82.   Each of the 50,000 records has an address or specific location on a disk of the storage unit of the computer.

In this application, the equivalent of 62,500 eighty-column punched cards, or 5,000,000 characters, is stored in the storage device of the computer. A total of 50,000 different records of 100 characters each constitutes the master information and previous balances. These 50,000 are prorated among the types of basic information and constitute addresses or identities by which specific records can be located by the computer. This is shown graphically by Figure 82.

The Processing by Computer.   For programming the cum system, each part contained in the bill of materials for each model has a parts record stored in a separate section in the computer. For example, the parts record for a purchased part contains the part number; the percentage allowance for loss, waste, or spoilage; the origin; the cum receipts; and the balance due on open purchase orders.

For the given period of 13 weeks, a master schedule or sales forecast by week by models is punched on a tape which is fed into the computer. This schedule is first processed by the bill-of-material section, or portion showing the materials needed. The computer calculates requirements by periods, namely, by multiplying usage by schedule by shrinkage factor. Next, the schedule period is adjusted for lead time on each piece part. These data are carried forward to the parts record, where they are stored awaiting information from other models. As this information from other models becomes available, it is combined with other like information so that the cum requirements by periods are accumulated on the parts record for each component. When and how much to purchase or make is determined by comparison of the accounts scheduled with the amounts available for each component as discussed above.

What was previously long, tedious labor required for inventory control is now accomplished in several hours by means of the computer. In addition, it is now a simple matter radically to revise the production program. Information can be quickly obtained regarding the position materialwise if a new production plan is attempted. Shortages and excesses of materials are pointed out, and the status of all components is revealed.

COMPUTER PROCESS CONTROL (CPC)

One more category of computer applications will be discussed. This application is computer process control (CPC), whereby the computer starts actions and acts upon the results of such actions, thus, in essence, allowing complete automation of the production line. Under this arrangement, the computer makes a running analysis of the process and compensates for changes as they occur. The general arrangement followed is graphically represented by Figure 83.

The computer is connected to many and various instruments which provide pertinent readings on variables critical to the process. These readings are analyzed, related, and processed at fantastic speeds, thus recording if the process is progressing satisfactorily or what, if any, part of the production process needs remedial action. If the latter is the case, the computer dispatches back through the communicative network a series of actions that cause individual controls on various pieces of production equipment to make necessary adjustments.

Different processes put different demands upon CPC. Chemical industries typically require a large number of calculations; other industries may necessitate relatively few checks, but they must be made with great rapidity. Complete CPC may cost upward of $1 million, depending upon

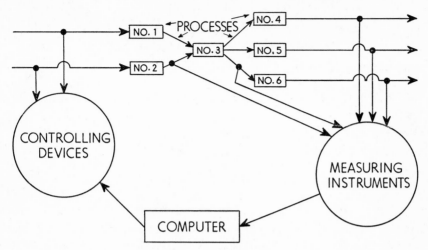

FIG. 83.   The general arrangement for computer process control (CPC).

the complexity of the process. But CPC can be achieved by stages, starting with the computer being used, not as an integral part of the process, but to assist human operators who have complete control of the manufacturing process. Gradually more and more control is given the computer.

Illustrative of CPC is the adaption of blast furnace operations in steel mills to computer control. This arrangement is an off-line application and enables the blast furnace operators to know the ideal and exact conditions for the most efficient operations for producing the best-quality finished product. Indications of difficulties and mechanical failures are detected in advance. A typical blast furnace consumes daily 4,800 tons of raw materials, mainly iron ore, limestone, and coke, and turns out 1,700 tons of iron. The grade of ore, quality of limestone, amount of heat, iron composition and purity desired, and a host of other variables are representative of the type of information which must be properly coordinated to operate the furnace in keeping with predetermined goals.

CONCLUSIONS ON COMPUTERS

Whatever the use of the computer, it is essential to keep in mind what is to be accomplished—what the real need of the enterprise or the office is. This is fundamental. The better approach might be to analyze and know the needs thoroughly, then get the machines that will best do the required work. On the other hand, knowing the machines and what can be done with them can prove a satisfactory approach. With machine knowledge as a background, it might be possible to adjust the procedures, and the form and type of records determined as essential, to fit what the machine can perform most economically. However, in either event, the real need of the enterprise in terms of its paper work requirements should receive top priority.

To reiterate, office automation stimulates thinking of office work as a whole, not just of a component of it. All the papers and records should be considered—not simply the payroll records, or the inventory statistics, or the order-handling procedure, or research and development requirements. Automation is geared to volume. There must be a sufficient quantity of work; frequently, this means grouping the components and performing the work for all. The benefits of office automation are numerous; yet problems are entailed that require comprehension, much thought, and study. Difficult decisions must be made. Deeply entrenched habits and beliefs may have to be dispelled. The design of office papers may require revision, the retraining of office personnel may be needed, and an extensive educational job with nonoffice personnel and customers may have to be conducted. Office automation is an area in which a manager *must* manage.

Finally, remember that change is always taking place; the direction and degree of this change in the way paper work is accomplished is, and will inevitably be, modified by the computer. Everywhere, the tempo of technological advance has quickened. The need for more and more information is being accelerated. Discoveries not yet imagined will be made. In such an era, the computer will occupy a role of increasing importance in the hopeful advances of human progress. Properly understood and applied, the computer will assist man in employing his talent, his time, and his ideas most effectively in the pursuit of values which make man so distinctive and his accomplishments so significant.